Endorsements from the

'Brennan has 'done the Cardinal a service by ei
taken as an objective account of an enormous tra
  Brian Skinner, *Journal of the Australian Catholic Historical Society*

'The issues raised in this commentary are important ones for society. In the
aftermath of the Royal Commission, the #metoo movement, and recent develop-
ments in Canberra, many are rightly wondering how we can overcome the difficulties victims of sexual assault face in coming forward and being believed, and
how this can be balanced with the rights of those who are accused to be treated
fairly. These ongoing conversations will ensure Brennan's contributions on the
Pell case will remain relevant for years to come.'
  Michael McVeigh, *Australian Catholics*

'[R]eaders will find this book compelling. It brings together fourteen major articles, interviews and commentaries that Brennan produced from February 2019
to March 2021: an impressive record and highly recommended reading.
  Keith Windschuttle, *Quadrant*

'Ordinary Australians are deeply indebted to Frank Brennan. His magnificent
achievement is that he has secured, for us ordinary folk, the principles of law and
reason as they should apply in a free, democratic and just society.'
  Fr Tony Percy, *Catholic Voice*

'As a matter of record, alongside Keith Windschuttle's The Persecution of
George Pell, this book stands as an important corrective to the writings of Louise
Milligan, Melissa Davey and Lucie Morris-Marr. The conduct of the Victorian police is properly criticised. The case collapses when one understands how
cathedral sacristies work on a Sunday morning with solemn high Mass, about
which the police did not make even rudimentary inquiries.'
  Fr Brian Lucas, *Australasian Catholic Record*

'In this collection of his writings about George Cardinal Pell, this Jesuit lawyer
provides a damning account of how Victoria police went on a fishing expedition
to find charges that could be laid against Pell, how they failed to consider that
the complainant might in perfect sincerity have displaced memories of who had
in fact abused him, and completely failed to corroborate the accusations with the
many people who were at St. Patrick's Cathedral after High Mass on either of
those long ago days when the then Archbishop of Melbourne was imagined to
have committed those improbable crimes.'

  Peter Craven, *The Spectator*

Other books by Frank Brennan

Too Much Order with Too Little Law

Land Rights Queensland Style

Sharing the Country

One Land, One Nation

Legislating Liberty

The Wik Debate

Tampering with Asylum

Acting on Conscience

The 2015 Gasson Lectures

No Small Change

The People's Quest for Leadership in Church and State

Amplifying That Still, Small Voice

Dedicated

to

Those who seek truth, justice and healing

and

to

Those who have been denied them

CONNOR COURT PUBLISHING PTY LTD
PO Box 7257
Redland Bay QLD 4165
sales@connorcourt.com
www.connorcourtpublishing.com.au

ISBN: 9781922449535 (pbk.)

Printed in Australia

Picture Credits

Cardinal Pell on the steps of St Mary's Cathedral Sydney after celebrating Mass (front cover), Catholic Archdiocese of Sydney.

William Holman Hunt's painting *The scapegoat* on page 9, wikipedia commons.

The Three Different Routes on page 82, drawing by *The Catholic Weekly,* Sydney.

Contents

Introduction

When the criminal proceedings against Cardinal George Pell commenced in July 2017, Fran Kelly, after interviewing me at some length about the government's treatment of refugees on Manus Island, changed tack and asked me on ABC Radio National *Breakfast*: 'Do you have concerns about this case, regardless of the outcome, and how it's going to affect the church?' I answered: 'Fran, I think this case will be a test of all individuals and all institutions involved. All we can do is hope the outcome will be marked by truth, justice, healing, reconciliation and transparency. A huge challenge for my church and, yes, a lot will ride on this case. But what is absolutely essential is the law be allowed to do its work ... And let's hope there can be truth and justice for all individuals involved in these proceedings.'[1]

When it was announced that Pell's first trial would be subject to a suppression order prohibiting any reporting of the proceedings by the media, I suggested to Pell that he ask a retired County Court judge to monitor the proceedings so as to be able to provide accurate information about the trial once the suppression order was lifted. Pell got back to me and told me that his advisers thought I would be a more appropriate person to discharge that role as I 'would go over better with the literati and the glitterati'. My principal concern was that members of the public, and particularly Catholics, were entitled to accurate information about the closed proceedings. I could not see that such accuracy and lack of bias would be provided by the group of journalists who were already circling. The books by Louise Milligan, Melissa Davey and Lucie Morris-Marr have confirmed my assessment.

By exchange of letters amongst the President and Vice President of the Australian Catholic Bishops Conference and my Jesuit provincial, I was asked 'to offer commentary on the conduct of the (Pell court)

---

[1]   Listen at https://www.abc.net.au/radionational/programs/breakfast/
       did-the-federal-government-break-promises-in-refugee/8740182

proceedings once the suppression orders have been lifted', noting that 'Any commentary needs to be seen, as much as is possible, to be clear, objective and impartial'.

In the first trial, the jury could not agree. So a second trial was ordered. Having attended some of these trials in the County Court and (unlike the journalists) having access to the transcript of proceedings (other than the complete evidence of the complainant), I published only one article which was republished a number of times after first appearing in *The Australian* when the suppression order was lifted (Chapter 1).

I gave three follow-up interviews: one to ABC *7.30* (Chapter 2); one to ABC *Drive Melbourne* (Chapter 3); and one to *Sky News* (Chapter 4). I posted a response to criticisms of my *Australian* article on Facebook (Chapter 5). I then said I would offer no further public comment until all legal proceedings were complete.

In March 2019, I attended the splendid exhibition at the National Gallery of Australia in Canberra, entitled 'Love and Desire: Pre-Raphaelite Masterpieces from the Tate'. I was captivated by William Holman Hunt's painting *The scapegoat* 1854–55 which the exhibition commentary described as 'a strangely compelling, uncanny image. In this first and smaller of two oil paintings the rainbow, mountainous landscape, dramatic atmospheric light and glowing moon all suggest a romanticised view. Yet we know this scene is far from paradise. Centre-stage – and commanding our attention – the gasping, shaggy-haired goat looks directly at the viewer as it appears to sink into the Dead Sea. Drawn from the Old Testament scripture of Leviticus, the sacrificial goat is the carrier of the sins of the world. We know from the ibex on the left, with just its head and long horns protruding from the sea, and from the deceased camel at right, that the scapegoat is not long for this world.'

I knew something of Pell's agony and despair. I maintained hope that the Australian legal system would deliver justice and that the superior courts would put right such an obvious injustice. I was to be disappointed by the two most senior judges in Victoria but was

8

sustained by the cogently argued dissent by Justice Mark Weinberg, the nation's most experienced criminal appeals judge. My hope was not to be vindicated for another year. Pell spent 404 days in prison.

I maintained my silence until the full bench of the High Court of Australia unanimously (7-0) ordered on 7 April 2020 that Pell's 'convictions be quashed and judgments of acquittal be entered in their place'.

I published three further articles about the proceedings. Immediately the High Court determined the matter in Cardinal Pell's favour, I published an article in *The Australian* explaining the judgment on 7 April 2020 (Chapter 6). Next day I preached on the statements issued by Cardinal Pell and the complainant (Chapter 7).

I wrote an article for the UK Catholic paper *The Tablet* explaining the case and its context to the international Catholic audience (Chapter 8). I then wrote a lengthy piece for *The Weekend Australian* outlining forensically the failures of the Victoria Police and the Director of Public Prosecutions (DPP) in this prosecution which should never have been brought (Chapter 9). I gave only one interview on this occasion, and it was to *Sky News*. The transcript is Chapter 10.

In all these pieces, I attempted to confine my public remarks to lessons to be learnt from the conduct of the trials by the Victoria Police and the DPP. I hope my comments will be an aid to fairer, less traumatic legal proceedings in future, for the wellbeing of victims, bona fide complainants and accused persons inappropriately charged.

Some of those disappointed by Pell's unanimous acquittal of all charges by the High Court claimed that he was acquitted on a technicality. Nothing could be further from the truth. The High Court, like the Victorian judges of the Court of Appeal, proceeded on the assumption that the jury found complainant J's evidence 'thoroughly credible and reliable'. All seven High Court justices, like Justice Weinberg in the court below, were convinced that 'the compounding improbabilities caused by the unchallenged evidence' of many other witnesses called by the prosecution 'whose honesty was not in question' 'required the jury, acting rationally, to have entertained a doubt about the applicant's guilt.'[2]

When you study the route and timing for the complainant's entry to the priests' sacristy, you can appreciate that there was no time when Pell, the complainant J and his companion could have been alone together in the priests' sacristy soon after the solemn Sunday mass. There was no time and place when and where Pell, J and his companion could be alone together for the 5-6 minutes needed for the first lot of offences to occur. This is just one of 'the compounding improbabilities' which required any jury acting rationally to acquit.

My refutation of the claim that the acquittal was made merely on a technicality was provided to some lawyers and commentators. It is Chapter 11. The author Melissa Davey who followed the trials made the preposterous claim that the lawyers for the prosecution and for defence who heard the complainant give his evidence had told her that he was 'eloquent, articulate, honest'. There is no way that the lawyers would have said any such thing to a journalist. I corrected this misapprehension (Chapter 12).

---

[2]   *Pell* v *The Queen* [2020] HCA 12 (7 April 2020), paras119-20, available at http://eresources.hcourt.gov.au/showCase/2020/HCA/12

Unlike the original trials, the proceedings in the Victorian Court of Appeal and in the High Court of Australia were not subject to any suppression order, so there was no need for me to give further interviews. I know the hurt caused to victims whenever a Catholic priest speaks on this issue. It is for others to provide an accessible analysis of the undoubtedly correct High Court decision, as well as informed critique of the demonstrably wrong decision by the Victorian Chief Justice and the President of the Victorian Court of Appeal. The Pell prosecution has revealed deep-seated problems in the Victorian criminal justice system.

In October 2020, Pope Francis, with great publicity and fanfare, received Cardinal Pell in an official audience at the Vatican. I provided Australian Jesuits with an assessment of the case made against Pell by the royal commission, concluding that the pope would have been briefed that the findings of the royal commission were questionable, its reasoning demonstrating a bias against Pell. That assessment is Chapter 13.

The Irish Jesuit journal *Studies: An Irish Quarterly Review* asked me: 'Where Has Cardinal Pell's Case Brought Us in the Australian Church?' My answer published in the Irish journal is Chapter 14.

Hopefully, this is my last word on the Pell proceedings, a dark chapter in Victorian legal history. I continue to hope and pray that all persons affected by these harrowing proceedings, most especially the complainant J and the defendant George Pell, can find some semblance of truth, justice, healing, reconciliation and transparency in the final outcome. The failures of the Victoria police, prosecution authorities, and the two most senior Victorian judges in these proceedings did nothing to help the efforts being made to address the trauma of institutional child sexual abuse. As a society we need to do better, and the legal system needs to play its part.

Fr Frank Brennan SJ AO
Newman College, University of Melbourne
7 April 2021, first anniversary of the High Court decision in *Pell* v *The Queen*

Introduction to the Second Edition

On the day of publication of the book, I published an opinion piece in *The Australian* entitled, 'I'm a critic but George Pell really was treated unjustly' (Chapter 15). I then gave one only interview on Sky News (Chapter 16). I delivered the annual Thomas More Oration in Canberra highlighting lessons for Church and State (Chapter 17). The one and only planned book launch had to be cancelled due to the pandemic. In its place, *The Catholic Weekly* published my remarks under the heading 'The Anatomy of a Vendetta' (Chapter 18).

Observations after the Jury Conviction

1

Father Frank Brennan on Cardinal George Pell guilty verdict: 'I still hope for truth, justice'

The Australian

26 February 2019

The suppression order in relation to Cardinal George Pell has been lifted. In December, a jury of twelve of his fellow citizens found him guilty of five offences of child sexual abuse. No other charges are to proceed. Cardinal Pell has appealed the convictions. The verdict was unanimous. The jury took three days to deliberate after a four-week trial. The trial was in fact a re-run. At the first trial, the jury could not agree. The trial related to two alleged victims, one of whom had died.

Members of the public could attend those proceedings if they knew where to go in the Melbourne County Court. Members of the public could hear all the evidence except a recording of the complainant's evidence from the first trial. The complainant, who cannot be identified, did not give evidence at the retrial; the recording from the first trial was admitted as the complainant's evidence. The recording was available to the public only insofar as it was quoted by the barristers in their examination of other witnesses or in their final addresses to the jury, and by the judge in his charge to the jury. So, no member of the public has a complete picture of the evidence and no member of the public is able to make an assessment of the complainant's demeanour. The complainant's evidence at the first trial lasted two and a half days. He had been cross-examined for more than a day by Cardinal Pell's defence barrister, Robert Richter QC who has a reputation for being one of the best and one of the toughest cross-examiners in the legal profession. Pell did not give evidence but a record of his police interview, denying the allegations, was in evidence.

The complainant's evidence related to events that occurred back in 1996 or 1997 when he was a thirteen-year-old choir boy at St Patrick's Cathedral Melbourne. Most other witnesses, had been choir boys, altar servers or Cathedral officials in 1996 when Pell first became archbishop of Melbourne. The complainant claimed that the first event, involving four charges, occurred after a solemn Sunday Mass celebrated by Archbishop Pell in the second half of 1996. It was common ground between the prosecution and the defence that the dates to which these four charges must be attributed were 15 December 1996 or 22 December 1996. These were the dates on which the first and second solemn Sunday Masses were celebrated by Archbishop Pell in the Cathedral after he had become archbishop in August 1996. The Cathedral had been undergoing renovations and thus was not used for Sunday Masses during earlier months of 1996.

The complainant said that he and another choir boy left the liturgical procession at the end of one Sunday Mass and went fossicking in the off-limits sacristy where they started swilling altar wine. The archbishop arrived unaccompanied, castigated them, and then, while fully robed in his copious liturgical vestments proceeded to commit three vile sexual acts including oral penetration of the complainant. The complainant said that the sacristy door was wide open and altar servers were passing along the corridor. The complainant said that he and the other boy then returned to choir practice. The choir was making a Christmas recording at that time.

These two choir boys stayed in the choir another year but, the complainant said, they never spoke about the matter to each other, even though they sometimes had sleepovers at each other's homes. The second boy was once asked by his mother if he had ever been abused by anybody and he said he had not.

The complainant claimed that a month or so later, after a Sunday Mass when the Archbishop was presiding (but not celebrating the Mass), Pell came along the corridor outside the sacristy where many choristers and others were milling about. He claimed that Pell grabbed him briefly, put him against the wall, and firmly grasped his genitalia. This was the subject of the fifth charge. Pell knew neither boy and had no contact with either of them thereafter.

The prosecution case was that Pell at his first or second solemn Sunday Mass as archbishop decided for some unknown reason to abandon the procession and his liturgical assistants and hasten from the Cathedral entrance to the sacristy unaccompanied by his Master of Ceremonies Monsignor Charles Portelli while the liturgical procession was still concluding. Portelli and the long time sacristan Max Potter described how the archbishop would be invariably accompanied after a solemn Mass with procession until one of them had assisted the archbishop to divest in the sacristy. There was ample evidence that the Archbishop was a stickler for liturgical form and that he developed strict protocols in his time as archbishop, stopping at the entrance to the Cathedral after Mass to greet parishioners usually for 10 to 20 minutes, before returning to the sacristy to disrobe in company with his Master of Ceremonies. The prosecution suggested that these procedures might not have been in place when Pell first became archbishop. The suggestion was that other liturgical arrangements might have been under consideration.

In his final address, Richter criticised inherent contradictions and improbabilities of many of the details of this narrative. I heard some of the publicly available evidence and have read most of the transcript. I found many of Richter's criticisms of the narrative very compelling. Anyone familiar with the conduct of a solemn Cathedral Mass with full choir would find it most unlikely that a bishop would, without grave reason, leave a recessional procession and retreat to the sacristy unaccompanied.

Witnesses familiar with liturgical vestments had been called who gave compelling evidence that it was impossible to produce an erect penis through a seamless alb. An alb is a long robe, worn under a heavier chasuble. It is secured and set in place by a cincture which is like a tightly drawn belt. An alb cannot be unbuttoned or unzipped, the only openings being small slits on the side to allow access to trouser pockets underneath. The complainant's initial claim to police was that Pell had parted his vestments, but an alb cannot be parted; it is like a seamless dress. Later the complainant said that Pell moved the vestments to the side. An alb secured with a cincture cannot be moved to the side. The police never inspected the vestments during their investigations, nor did the prosecution show that the vestments could be parted or moved to the side as the complainant had alleged. The proposition that the offences charged were committed immediately after Mass by a fully robed Archbishop in the sacristy with an open door and in full view from the corridor seemed incredible to my mind.

I was very surprised by the verdict. In fact, I was devastated. My only conclusion is that the jury must have disregarded many of the criticisms so tellingly made by Richter of the complainant's evidence and that, despite the complainant being confused about all manner of things, the jury must nevertheless have thought – as the recent royal commission discussed - that children who are sexually violated do not always remember details of time, place, dress and posture. Although the complainant got all sorts of facts wrong, the jury must have believed that Pell did something dreadful to him. The jurors must have judged the complainant to be honest and reliable even though many of the details he gave were improbable if not impossible.

Cardinal Pell has been in the public spotlight for a very long time. There are some who would convict him of all manner of things in the court of public opinion no matter what the evidence. There are others who would never convict him of anything, holding him in the highest regard. The criminal justice system is intended to withstand these preconceptions. The system is under serious strain, however, when it comes to Cardinal Pell.

The events of the Victorian parliamentary inquiry, the federal royal commission, the publication of Louise Milligan's book *Cardinal* and Tim Minchin's song *Come Home (Cardinal Pell)* were followed, just two weeks before the trial commenced, by the Parliamentary apology to the victims of child sexual abuse. The Prime Minister Scott Morrison said, 'Not just as a father, but as a Prime Minister, I am angry too at the calculating destruction of lives and the abuse of trust, including those who have abused the shield of faith and religion to hide their crimes, a shield that is supposed to protect the innocent, not the guilty. They stand condemned... on behalf of the Australian people, this Parliament and our government... I simply say I believe you, we believe you, your country believes you.' Such things tend to shift not the legal, but the reputational, burden upon an accused person to prove innocence rather than the prosecution to prove guilt.

Would the verdict have been different if Pell had given evidence? Who can tell? All one can say is that, although the defence seemed to be on strong ground in submitting that the circumstances made the narrative advanced by the prosecution manifestly improbable, that failed to secure the acquittal.

Was the verdict unreasonable? Can it be supported having regard to the evidence? Those are questions for the appeal court. I can only hope and pray that the complainant can find some peace, able to get on with his life, whichever way the appeal goes. Should the appeal fail, I hope and pray that Cardinal Pell, heading for prison, is not the unwitting victim of a wounded nation in search of a scapegoat. Should the appeal succeed, the Victoria Police should review the adequacy of the police investigation of these serious criminal charges.

When the committal proceedings against Cardinal Pell first commenced in July 2017, Fran Kelly asked me on ABC Radio National Breakfast: 'Do you have concerns about this case, regardless of the outcome, and how it's going to affect the Church?' I answered: 'Fran,

I think this case will be a test of all individuals and all institutions involved. And all we can do is hope that the outcome will be marked by truth, justice, healing, reconciliation and transparency. A huge challenge for my church, and yes a lot will ride on this case. But what is absolutely essential is that the law be allowed to do its work. And let's wait and see the evidence, and let's wait and see how it plays out. And let's hope there can be truth and justice for all individuals involved in these proceedings.' And that is still my hope.

2

Transcript of ABC *7.30* Interview with Leigh Sales[1]

26 February 2019

LEIGH SALES, PRESENTER: Supporters of George Pell believe he's been wrongly convicted, but even for Catholics who accept the verdict, it's a devastating outcome - yet another blow to the trust and faithfulness of Catholic parishioners around the world.

Father Frank Brennan is a Jesuit priest, professor of law and CEO of Catholic Social Services Australia.

Frank Brennan, you have written today that you are very surprised by the verdict and, in fact, devastated. Why?

FR FRANK BRENNAN, JESUIT PRIEST AND LAWYER: Well, my devastation is as a Catholic in contemporary Australia, that Cardinal Pell, who is the most senior church leader we've had in this country, has been found guilty of child sexual abuse in the most horrific of circumstances and even after a solemn mass, surprised in that I did sit in on some of the trial, and I have read a fair bit of the transcript, and of course, I, like members of the public have not heard the victim himself, and I'm aware that he gave evidence over some days, and he was closely cross-examined by Robert Richter, who is said to be a very good cross-examiner who was appearing for Cardinal Pell and the jury has found Cardinal Pell guilty and that, in a trial where it seemed to me, there were quite a number of improbabilities in relation

---

[1]　Available at https://www.abc.net.au/7.30/father-frank-brennan-on-the-convic-tion-of-george/10851858

to the evidence, but nonetheless, 12 conscientious Australian citizens off the street have said we're convinced beyond reasonable doubt that this happened.

LEIGH SALES: So do you accept that verdict then?

FRANK BRENNAN: I accept the verdict, being a lawyer, subject to any appeals process, of course.

LEIGH SALES: What did you think were the improbabilities?

FRANK BRENNAN: Well, the improbabilities for someone familiar with the way a mass works in the cathedral led by an Archbishop, were basically that what was alleged by the prosecution was that at his first or second public solemn high mass in St Patrick's Cathedral, Cardinal Pell came out on the front steps where he had a long procession in front of him of choristers, servers, that sort of thing, and instead of doing what became undoubtedly, his usual practice of spending 10 or 15 minutes on the steps talking to people, and instead of being accompanied by his master of ceremonies, which inevitably is done in those sorts of events, it's a bit like a military parade, having people properly escorted, that Pell decided for some unknown reason to go off on his own, back into the sacristy, where he then found the two choirboys swilling altar wine, and then with the door of the sacristy open, where a lot of people are milling around after a mass of that sort, that then fully vested, he had his way with them in a most horrific fashion, and that then the two boys withdrew.

They didn't speak about it with each other again. They stayed in the choir for another year, and all of that was highlighted by Richter as being improbabilities.

But of course, these were matters for the jury, Leigh, and I readily concede, I, like members of the public, I have not heard the victim give his evidence.

I know he was subjected to cross-examination by Richter for over a day and, of course, Cardinal Pell himself did not give evidence.

LEIGH SALES: If Pell had gone to a priest and confessed these acts, that priest under the sanctity of the confessional would keep that a secret.

Is that in line with acceptable community standards today?

FRANK BRENNAN: No, it's not, and that's why at the moment I think the discussion in the Catholic Church is as to what is the appropriate way to conduct the sacrament of confession.

In the Catholic tradition, we have a number of ways. We have what is called a third rite, which can be a communal right where there isn't a personal confession of sin, and I would think in these sorts of circumstances we'll have to move towards that, if we retain the sacrament in any real sense.

LEIGH SALES: We know the church hierarchy has some soul-searching to do in the wake of this verdict and so forth, but I wonder just for the ordinary lay person in the Catholic Church who looks at this and looks at everything that happens, and feels betrayed and let down, and even perhaps rattled in their own faith, what would be your message to them?

FRANK BRENNAN: Absolutely, and that it's devastating for all of us, including people like myself.

Priests give their life full-time to the show, and that basically we're in an institution at the moment where the highest membership of it has been found guilty of an offence of this sort.

Now, I don't think I'm being trite in saying even if the processes of the law were to show that the verdict were unsafe, and that won't be a matter for me, that's a matter for an appeal court, and I passionately believe in our legal system as well as the church, but even if that happens, we're all left with the realisation that 12 decent Australians off the street listening to the evidence of the victim and listening to everything that was outlined, including the improbabilities, say we are absolutely convinced that Cardinal Pell did something dreadful to this young man and his companion.

That leaves us with a leadership which in terms of public credibility has been absolutely shattered.

Now what that calls us back to is the core of the Christian message and not a lot of the Roman superstructure.

LEIGH SALES: Frank Brennan, thank you very much for speaking to us this evening.

FRANK BRENNAN: Thank you, good to be with you.

3

Transcript of interview with Rafael Epstein on ABC *Drive Melbourne*[2]

26 February 2019

RE: Father Frank Brennan is a respected legal commentator. He's a Jesuit priest; he's also CEO of Catholic Social Services Australia and he sat through some of the trial and he had access to much of the transcript. He's in our Sydney studio. Thanks for joining us.

FB: Hello Raf. It's good to be with you.

RE: You wrote today that you were surprised by the verdict. Why?

FB: Well I was surprised as a lawyer but, you know, I don't think that this is the day to go into too much on that Raf. I was also very shocked by the verdict. As a Catholic in contemporary Australia, to think that the highest ranking church official in our church has being found guilty of an offence of this sort, is truly shocking for all of us. And whatever I might think about the particular improbabilities in the evidence in the case, I like any one has to admit that I have not heard the evidence of the victim. We will never hear his evidence under the rules that exist. And we know that the victim was cross examined for over a day by Robert Richter, the lawyer for Cardinal Pell. And we know that Richter is a very accomplished cross-examiner. And what

2   Available at https://soundcloud.com/frank-brennan-6/interview-with-raf-ep-stein-abc-melbourne

we're left with at the end of the day is that 12 decent Australians off the street as jurors have said that they are convinced beyond reasonable doubt that Cardinal Pell did these dreadful things to this victim and his mate.

So having said that, yes there are aspects of the evidence that were then included in statements in the final addresses and in the charge by the judge which would have people who know how a mass runs where it is said that Cardinal Pell did these dreadful things straight after a solemn high mass in the cathedral in the sacristy, where there would have been people milling around and all that sort of thing, that those sorts of improbabilities are there. But the good thing about our legal system is we've got the appeal system which can determine whether the verdict is a safe verdict, and if it is then we all live with those consequences.

RE: So what I'm hearing Fr Brennan, I mean this with the greatest of respect, I just want to sum up what I think you're trying to say: you have personal issues where you feel some of the evidence didn't quite support a conviction; at the same time, you're a lawyer - twelve members of the jury heard it. Cardinal Pell's defence lawyer had a go. So you've got personal issues I guess with the evidence. But you're a big believer in the justice system, and you think it's delivered. Is that fair?

FB: Yes. I'm a great believer in the justice system. I say, let the appeal process play itself out, and yes, if he is found guilty, this will be a tragic realisation particularly for those of us in the Catholic Church who thought it was almost inconceivable that someone in that position would do things of this sort particularly after a solemn High Mass in the cathedral.

RE: Yes. You also wrote that you're worried that the burden might have shifted in some way, that someone has to prove their innocence.

FB: Yes, I think it's fair to say that in a case of this sort with Cardinal Pell that he's become a person of such notoriety that I think he carried a lot in terms of having to prove things and of course one of the facts about this case is that Cardinal Pell did not give evidence, and I presume that was a decision of him and his lawyers. Now that being the case, and I could imagine to myself some jurors saying to themselves, 'Well, God help us, after everything we've been through with the Royal Commission and all the rest of it, we've had enough of the Catholic Church paying lots of money to employ flash lawyers and then sitting there silent.' I think all of those sorts of factors could have been at play. That's all I'm saying.

RE: What do you say to people who are Catholic who feel that they doubt the moral authority of the Church more today?

FB: Well I readily understand it. I mean Cardinal Pell has occupied absolutely the highest position, and let's put it at its absolute minimum: what you've got is a situation where someone who was so respected in the Catholic hierarchy as to get up there as Number 3 next to the Pope, when he appears before 12 of his fellow citizens, he is found beyond reasonable doubt in their minds to have committed the most dreadful offences.

RE: Does the Catholic Church still have moral authority?

FB: I think it's very reduced. I do think the Church has moral authority when it stands up for the right things in terms of the gospel, particularly when it stands up for people who are poor and marginalised. But when it just tries to dictate its own agenda, I think in a society like Australia now it has next to none.

RE: Next to no moral authority?

FB: Yes, when it comes to defending simply its own position. But when we're out there doing the hard yards for people who are marginalised and disempowered, then I think we do have moral authority, and I think we as a society should hang onto it.

RE: There's been a lot of discussion in the Vatican this week. They've also defrocked a man who was Archbishop of Washington DC . I think that's been much more rapid than in the past. Do you think the Vatican gets it?

FB: When you say the Vatican, then obviously there's the Pope and then there are the Cardinals and all the people and the dicasteries etc. I think this Pope is trying desperately hard. He's doing his best to try and make sure that the Vatican as you say gets it. Let me put it this way: the bind he's in is that he came from South America very committed to a papacy different from that of John Paul II. He didn't want all the centralised power where he simply issued dictates out of Rome. He wanted local bishops' conferences to take more responsibility. I think that's why he called together all the heads of bishops' conferences from around the world, saying to them that it's not just for me or the Vatican to get it; it's also for all of you to get it and to get back in your own local cultural contexts and to do something about it.

RE: Do you think there are significant issues with the Catholic Church in places like Africa, South America, Asia, where there are not many figures like yourself?

FB: I'm sure there are. But it's not a matter of having figures like myself Raf. There are places where churches and other institutions have not had things like a five year Royal Commission as we had here in Australia. I have long said in the lead up to the Royal Commission that the church needed the help of the state in order to deal with these issues. It's one of the things I'm proud of, I have to say Raf. I'm a person with double allegiances. I believe in the church. I also believe in our legal institutions. And that's why I see this Cardinal Pell trial as so critical. It's absolutely essential that the law be got right, and then it's absolutely essential that we learn the lessons from whatever flows from this case.

RE: Just finally Frank Brennan: how did you feel today? I've only got 30 seconds until the news. How did you feel this morning?

FB: I felt dreadful but of course I have known about the verdict for some time because I was there in the court. But I felt, well here is the moment of reckoning for the Australian Catholic Church, confronting what is just an enormous curse which has been hanging over us. And I felt: let's hope this can be a day for the victims because, and I don't know the victims down there in Ballarat, two things have happened today and let's not forget

RE: Very briefly.

FB: Those who were victims in Ballarat have been told no cases in Ballarat will go forward ever. And then in relation to the incident in the cathedral, we have a finding now which will be appealed.

RE: Really appreciate your time. That's Fr Frank Brennan. You can hear that he is a lawyer, Jesuit priest, and CEO of Catholic Social Services Australia, and very honest there. He's got a lengthy explanation in *The Australian* newspaper of his concerns with the trial, but also saying that in some respects the Australian church has almost zero moral authority in this country.

4

'The Law Needs to Run Its Course', Interview with Kieran Gilbert and Laura Jayes[3]

Sky News

27 February 2019

KG: Joining us now is lawyer, academic, and Jesuit priest Father Frank Brennan. Father Frank, thanks for your time. You have attended a number of the hearings and read a lot of the testimony in this case. Today in *The Australian* you write that you were devastated and surprised by the verdict. Can you elaborate this morning for our viewers?

FB: Yes, well all of us have to accept that either George Pell did this or he didn't and either way it's absolutely devastating. But in terms of the trial what we all have to accept, we members of the public, we don't have access directly to the evidence given by the victim but all we have is what is referred to of his evidence by the various lawyers and by the judge in the final charge and in matters that were put to other witnesses. And I think it's fair to say that there were quite a number of improbabilities as Pell's lawyer described that. At the end of the day what we're left with is a jury verdict which was unanimous, where clearly a jury was of the view that George Pell did dreadful things to this victim and to his mate. But we live under the rule of law. There will be an appeal and I think it appropriate that absolute final

---

[3] Video available at https://www.skynews.com.au/details/_6007490868001

verdict be held until that appeal is dealt with.

LJ: Father, today you write that I hope and pray that Pell who is likely heading for prison at this stage is not the unwitting victim of a nation in search of a scapegoat. Two things here: do you think he is a scapegoat? do you think that as a nation after all these accusations that have been put forward this is what we're after?

FB: I don't know Laura is the short answer. Basically, I think there are three classes of citizens when we look at George Pell. There are those who hate him and those who hate the Catholic Church; they would believe anything that was said against him. There are those who think that George Pell is absolutely wonderful, and they love the Catholic Church and they don't think that George Pell could ever do anything wrong. There are then the vast majority of us who say we just don't know. We believe in a legal system where there is need for justice and transparency. Now what I'm suggesting there is this: if George Pell did these things then yes this is truly dastardly that I am part of a church where someone like that could be promoted to number 3 having done such dreadful things against children and straight after a solemn high mass. So that's appalling. If he didn't do these things, then equally it's appalling that we live in a society where there can be such demonisation and scapegoating. Now it's one or the other. So either way, this is a truly dreadful situation for all of us to be in at this time.

KG: You go through the hearings and some of the evidence or lack thereof as you've written this morning including the testimony from the victim as well which was actually not given in person at this particular hearing, was it?

FB: No, the way it works under Victorian law and it's designed to protect victims and that's very understandable is that the victim gives evidence by videolink into the court so not to see the accused person and so as not to be subjected to the trauma of being there in the courtroom. But because in this case in the first trial the jury could not agree, then there was a need for a retrial. And under Victorian law instead of putting the victim through the trauma of giving the evidence over again, the jury simply sits there and watches the video for three or four days of what was done during the first trial. So I imagine (of course not being allowed to be in the court to see it), but I imagine it's a slightly eerie experience having to watch a four-day video.

LJ: This is as you wrote today a test for all individuals and institutions.

FB: Absolutely.

LJ: What does this now mean for the church, Father Frank, because in recent times there's a lot of people who have lost faith in the institution, the church. Have you lost any faith in your own institution? I guess it goes back to that previous question, you know, A or B that it could be here.

FB: What's fundamental for those of us who are Catholic is we are fundamentally Christian, and yes, we live it out according to the rites of the Catholic Church. But I think we all have to accept, even those who are the most heart on sleeve Catholics, that the Catholic Church in the western world as an institution which is managed and directed by a group of unmarried men, those days have gone because such a class is seen to be completely out of touch with what is just the daily normal lived experience of people. So I think there is a need for fundamental change particularly ensuring the place of women at the table. I say that because we had I think a very good Truth Justice and Healing Council of the Catholic Church during the Royal Commission. There were half a dozen women on that council and they not only did a fabulous job. All you have to do is read what they said in their reports to find a way forward. So I think there is a need for fundamental root and branch reform.

KG: Are you comfortable with the way the Vatican has handled this particular conviction that any final decision by the Pope, the Holy See, will be made pending that final appeal?

FB: Yes, I'm quite comfortable with that because what the Vatican has done, the same as they did with Philip Wilson, is withdraw the individual from all public ministry the moment the charges are there. And that's been appropriately done with Pell. And yes, with a bit of Roman deliberation, it was decided to take him out of the equation of every role there at the Vatican once this case was underway. So there is no way that he is allowed to exercise any ministry. Then we come to the question: well what about any sanctions to be imposed by the church? Now I think everyone, even Pell's greatest enemies in Australia should concede: well let the law take its course; let the appeals take their course; and if this is found to be an unsafe verdict, let's do a recalibration. If it's found not to be an unsafe verdict, then that is the time for the church to proceed with its own canonical procedures and be sure of this: though Cardinal Pell did not give evidence in these civil proceedings, I am sure he will give evidence before any church proceedings before there is a final determination whether to divest him of all positions and of his priesthood in the Catholic Church.

KJ: What do you say to everyone today including Christians who feel conflicted on this issue, feeling for the victims on one hand not wanting to diminish the conviction, but also their faith being shaken that Australia's highest Catholic has been convicted?

FB: I think we have to hold all that together Laura, and that's what I try to do publicly and privately. Let's make no mistake: yesterday, the victims learned a number of things. First there had been a number of allegations around the Ballarat pool or whatever. It was made clear by the Director of Public Prosecutions that there is absolutely no prospect of a trial being held in relation to those charges. They've fallen over. So there will be people in Ballarat who are feeling disappointed about that. Second, we then have this particular case where yes, I think a lot of people looking as objectively as they can at the little evidence that is available would be of the view that as I have said there are improbabilities. It is one thing to say yes, I believe what the victim has said. It's another thing to say that I'm convinced beyond reasonable doubt that this is what occurred even given the improbabilities. Now I am the first to acknowledge, as our Prime Minister did, that what we must do is believe victims and we know from the experts now, victims particularly when they're children, particularly when they're traumatised, there are all sorts of details they don't remember or that they get wrong. And so the real question for us is how do we believe victims in terms of the wrongs they've suffered while at the same time doing justice to someone against whom an allegation is made. Because we all know infallibility, it is very questionable now in the Catholic Church, but infallibility has never been a claim of the legal system. We're conflicted because all of us need to have a commitment to a robust legal system that does justice and does it transparently for all.

KG: Father Frank Brennan, we appreciate your time after a very difficult time for the Catholic church. Thank you for that.

FB: Thank you.

5

Facebook Post

7 March 2019

My article in *The Australian* on the Pell verdict (and reproduced elsewhere) has elicited quite a range of responses. I am sorry for any hurt caused to readers, particularly those who are victims of child sexual abuse.

I want to assure all readers that I wrote as I did because I thought there was a need for someone who had attended some of the proceedings and who had read the publicly available evidence to be in a position to state the issues which had arisen at trial and the issues likely to be raised on appeal.

Some readers have thought that I was questioning the honesty and truthfulness of the complainant. I did not, and I do not. I wrote (or at least, I intended to write) respecting the victim, respecting the jury, and respecting the legal processes including the appeal courts.

Given the suppression orders, the prior publicity, the perpetual non-disclosure of any complainant's evidence, and the likely public outcry once any suppression orders were lifted, I thought it responsible that I attempt to inform the public (and particularly concerned Catholics) about the legal complexities of the case, and as dispassionately as possible.

In such circumstances, justice and transparency demand a suspension of final judgment until an appeal court has had the opportunity to determine if the jury verdict is safe and reasonable. Such a suspension of final judgment is no disrespect to any victim nor to the jury nor to the legal processes.

I am acutely aware that anything said by a Catholic priest on these issues at this time will cause hurt to some people, and motivations etc will always be questioned. That's why I wrote only one article and gave only three interviews following the publication of my piece. I declined many requests for further interviews and opinion pieces.

Some have suggested that I should have said nothing at all. I respectfully disagree. That would have left the field largely to those journalists who attended the trial, some of whom have a limited understanding of the law, and some of whom display a lack of accuracy as they seek to paint their own picture of the proceedings.

I will give just one example which involves me directly, and which hopefully will not cause the least hurt to any reader. One of the journalists covering the proceedings most closely has been Lucie Morris-Marr. She has been covering the proceedings for CNN and *The New Daily*. She is to publish the big book on it all which will be published by Allen & Unwin in August 2019. On her website she states: 'most notably, Lucie was the first journalist in the world to reveal to the public and the Catholic community world-wide that there was a secret police investigation into the third most powerful figure in the Vatican – Cardinal George Pell – regarding allegations of historic sexual abuse.'

You'd hope she'd be accurate, at least about parts of the trial she claims to have witnessed. On 26 February 2019, Ms Marr published a piece entitled, 'Tantrum and tears: The moment the George Pell verdict was delivered'. It purports to be an eye witness account of the events in the court room on the afternoon of Tuesday 11 December 2018 when the jury delivered its verdict. She wrote: 'Pell's most high-profile supporter, former deputy prime minister Tim Fischer, had been at court to support Pell in the final days of the trial despite suffering from leukaemia. On that day he was absent.'But loyal supporters Katrina Lee, executive advisor from the Archdiocese of Sydney and human rights lawyer Father Frank Brennan remained poker-faced in their seats.'

I was not there that day. I wasn't even in Melbourne. I had not been in the courtroom since the previous Friday. I was not there on the Monday. I was not there on the Tuesday. On Monday, I was speaking at the National Library in Canberra with Michael Kirby et al marking the 70th anniversary of the UN Declaration of Human Rights. In the evening I was in the Parliament House studio in Canberra on the ABC *Drum* discussing the republic and indigenous recognition with Peter FitzSimons et al. On the Tuesday, I was attending to the work of Catholic Social Services in Canberra before driving to Bathurst to address 100 staff of CatholicCare. It was en route to Bathurst that I received a text message telling me of the verdict.

Imagine if we had to rely upon the likes of Ms Morris-Marr for our information. She claims to have seen me in the courtroom in Melbourne at the fateful moment when I was a thousand kilometres away. My being there helped her paint a journalistic picture. It just wasn't true.

Observations after the
High Court Acquittal

6

We Should be Grateful Justice has been delivered[4]

The Australian

8 April 2020

Some Australians, including many victims of child sexual abuse, revile George Pell. Others hold him in high esteem. Yesterday's High Court decision is unlikely to change personal views of the man but this judgment concerns everyone for it is about the administration of our criminal justice system for all, both accused and victims, in accordance with law.

The Pell saga has now run for over four years, ever since the Victoria Police commenced an operation on Christmas Eve 2015 seeking evidence of any wrongdoing by Pell around his cathedral during the years 1996-2001 when he was archbishop of Melbourne. This extraordinary trawling exercise turned up only one complainant whose allegations were taken all the way to trial. The complainant gave evidence that he and his now deceased companion were sexually assaulted by Pell in the priests' sacristy immediately after solemn Sunday mass in St Patrick's Cathedral in late 1996. He also gave evidence that Pell assaulted him in the sacristy corridor after another mass a couple of months later. That's the case that the High Court has just

---

[4]   Available at https://tinyurl.com/2wt2zvfb

thrown out. Thus the anger and relief at yesterday's decision.

The High Court has spoken definitively, unanimously and with one voice. The seven Justices have agreed that in relation to all five charges, 'there is a significant possibility that an innocent person has been convicted'. The court ordered that Pell's 'convictions be quashed and judgments of acquittal be entered in their place'. Pell will be able to celebrate mass at Easter. The complainant, having undergone extensive periods of stress, is left to get on with his life as best he can, wondering what was the point of this protracted legal trauma.

The court accepted that the jury had assessed the complainant's evidence 'as thoroughly credible and reliable'. In the Victorian Court of Appeal, that step was enough for two of the judges to uphold the convictions. But the dissenting judge, Mark Weinberg, Australia's most experienced criminal appeal court judge, thought that was only the first step of a court's inquiry, and not the last. All seven High Court judges agree. The court needed to examine the record of all the evidence in the case 'to see whether, notwithstanding that assessment, the court is satisfied that the jury, acting rationally, ought nonetheless to have entertained a reasonable doubt as to proof of guilt'. The court unanimously decided that any jury acting rationally must have had a reasonable doubt.

In addition to the complainant, there were many other witnesses called by the prosecution in Pell's case. They included 23 witnesses 'who were involved in the conduct of solemn Mass at the Cathedral or who were members of the choir in 1996 and/or 1997'. Many of these witnesses were also thoroughly credible and reliable, though their reliability faltered at times given that they were trying to recall what they would have been doing after mass in St Patrick's Cathedral on a particular Sunday 22 years before. The honesty of these witnesses was not questioned by the prosecution.

The High Court found that many of these witnesses had given consistent evidence that placed Pell on the steps of the Cathedral for at least 10 minutes after mass on 15 and 22 December 1996, the only possible dates when the first four offences could have been committed. The prosecution 'conceded that the offences alleged in the first incident could not have been committed if, following Mass, (Pell) had stood on the Cathedral steps greeting congregants for ten minutes.'

The court also found that there was unquestioned evidence by honest witnesses that placed Pell in company with his Master of Ceremonies when he returned to the priests' sacristy to disrobe. Furthermore there was abundant evidence of 'continuous traffic into and out of the priests' sacristy for ten to 15 minutes' after the altar servers returned to the sacristy at the end of the procession at the conclusion of mass. There was no 5-6 minute hiatus for the offences to occur with Pell, the complainant and his companion in the sacristy alone, together and uninterrupted, straight after mass.

The tragedy of this case for everyone, and especially for the complainant, is that a police investigation is expected to identify problems with a complainant's account. In this case it did not.

When interviewed in Rome back in October 2016 by Victorian police officers who were being supervised by their Deputy Commissioner Shane Patton, Pell told the police that the sacristy was 'a hive of activity' after mass with altar servers, sacristan, assistant sacristan, money collectors and any concelebrating priests coming and going. He said he would have been accompanied at all relevant times by his MC Charles Portelli.

The police returned to Australia and interviewed Portelli and the sacristan Max Potter who basically confirmed all that Pell had said about the 'hive of activity'. But the police did not bother to interview one single altar server. They made no inquiries about money collectors or concelebrating priests. They proceeded to charge Pell - with great media fanfare. They went ahead building a case on the basis that the priests' sacristy might have been left vacant and open on this one particular day – contrary to all church routine and ritual. Yet the High Court rightly observed that 'adherence to ritual and compliance with established liturgical practice is a defining feature of religious observance.'

The farce of the case was the belated attempt by the Director of Public Prosecutions to create the space for the necessary 5-6 minute hiatus. At trial, the prosecutor had suggested, contrary to the evidence, that the altar servers might have adjourned to another room, for no reason, for 5-6 minutes before being called back to the priests' sacristy to resume their duties at the end of mass. He had to withdraw that suggestion before the jury. In the High Court, the DPP submitted once again that the servers might have adjourned to another room or to the sanctuary to assist the sacristan. The High Court dealt with this suggestion kindly but firmly: 'The submission comes close to repeating the submission which the prosecutor withdrew at the trial. There was no evidence that the altar servers went to their room to disrobe prior to returning to the sanctuary in order to assist in clearing away the sacred vessels and other objects.'

In the end, there was just not the evidence to support the complainant's account. There never was. For the good of all victims and complainants, the Victorian Police and DPP need to review their procedures in cases like this. Those who neither canonise nor despise George Pell should be grateful that the High Court has finally delivered justice according to law in this protracted Victorian saga.

7

Sky News **Interview**
with Kieran Gilbert

8 April 2020[5]

Kieran Gilbert: Then for his thoughts on this case, a momentous case in the life of the Catholic Church in this country, Father Frank Brennan. And I want to start by just reading a line in your piece in *The Australian* today. You said those who neither canonised nor despise Pell should be grateful the High Court has delivered justice according to law in this protracted saga. Can you elaborate on that for our viewers this afternoon?

Frank Brennan: Yes, Kieran, I think in Australian society, there are basically three groups of people when it comes to Cardinal Pell. There are those who revile him. And it wouldn't matter what any court said, it wouldn't change their opinion. There are those who think he's absolutely wonderful and idolise or canonise him. And it wouldn't matter what any court said that wouldn't change their view. But then I think there's the vast majority of Australians who say, well, we want the processes of the law to work themselves through. If there is an allegation which is made against someone of his standing. And I think that's precisely what the High Court has done. The tragedy in this case, Kieran, is that the policing that was done by the Victoria Police in this particular case was very shoddy. The supervision of the brief by the Director of Public Prosecutions of Victoria was shoddy. The way

5   Video available at https://www.youtube.com/watch?v=1IH4Lg3ytnE

the Director of Public Prosecutions conducted herself, particularly in the High Court, was appalling. And so what we've had is a situation where it's been very difficult for people to get a ready resolution of matters.

Frank Brennan: The other thing Kieran in relation to the Victorian legal system is it's very clear this decision should have been reached by the Victorian Court of Appeal a year ago. On that court, which held two to one against Pell. The one dissentient was Mark Weinberg, who indisputably is the leading criminal appeal judge in the country. And the two in the majority who gave a judgment adverse to Pell, suffice to say that all seven of the High Court judges have basically indicated that their judgment was dreadful.

Kieran Gilbert: So, in that context, can you explain for those non-lawyers of us? When you read that High Court judgment, it basically made it clear that they accepted the complainant's evidence as credible on the basis of the jury's findings on that, that it was a credible witness. Now, in that sense, how does that equate with a seven-nil judgment of the full bench?

Frank Brennan: Quite easily, actually. And I've always thought this is a very simple case Kieran. So, what the seven High Court judges have said is this, look, when it comes to this complainant, we accept that the jury must have thought that he was credible and reliable. That means that you treat his evidence and you assess it without in any way saying, oh, maybe he was telling a fib or whatever. But as in any case, where you've got 23 witnesses as you had in this case, well, guess what? Of the other witnesses, most of them were also found to be very honest and credible. And they gave evidence about things where they had no skin in the game. They were simply offering recollections of what they would do during a service after mass in the cathedral.

See what the lay people have to remember about the legal processes in this case Kieran, is the trials were conducted under suppression orders, which meant that we ordinary mortals, we didn't have access to what was going on in the court day to day. So, in the end, all we got was the verdict that said he was guilty. And so it was only when the case came before the appeal courts where the first time members of the public could be looking at what was said, as to what actually occurred. And in this case, we know and I feel very deeply for the complainant in this case because I think the lesson to be learned is it was the stuff ups by the police and the DPP, which meant that this individual had to spend four years of his life undergoing additional trauma where his credible story could have been checked out by the police if they'd done their job.

Frank Brennan: Because back in October 2016, you had three Victorian police, including, God help us, the Deputy Commissioner of Police who flew to Rome in order that Pell be interviewed. Pell had been told, oh well, this is in relation to after choir around the cathedral. It was only during the record of interview that it was made clear to Pell that it was alleged that this occurred after Sunday Mass. Pell then in October 2016 said to them, well, that's impossible, because in the sacristy, after 11:00 am mass, there would be altar servers, there'd be the sacristan, there'd be the assistant sacristan. They'd be the people who come in who've collected the money and there'd been concelebrating Priests. He said go back to Australia and check all that out.

Well, guess what? The police never interviewed one altar server. The police never identified one concelebrating Priest. The police never sought out one money collector. These are the ordinary, decent Australians. Yes they happen to be Catholic, but they'd be just doing what they always do on a Sunday after mass. So this was the problem, Kieran, that what we had was a case where, yes, the prosecutor did his best to find the five or six minutes in that sacristy where he could get rid of the Master of Ceremonies, get rid of the altar servers, get rid of the money collectors, get rid of the concelebrants. But they just couldn't find the five or six minutes. And then God help us in the High Court of Australia, the Director of Public Prosecutions, in person, before the bench, basically created a story and created evidence to suggest that it was possible that these altar servers disappeared for five or six minutes into a room next door.

Frank Brennan: Now, the critical thing Kieran, is that that had been put by the Prosecutor to the jury at the trial. But when he was asked to withdraw that by the judge quite properly, because there was no evidence of it, he did it. And guess what happened in the High Court of Australia? The Director of Public Prosecutions with the QC sitting beside her, who had argued the case before the jury. She just threw him under the bus and said, oh, he shouldn't have made that concession.

Frank Brennan: And then she invented a piece of evidence as if to justify what was now being put as the argument. Now, of course, the High Court, all seven of them, you could see on their faces that this was just absolutely preposterous. And that's been the problem with this case Kieran. Sure. There's all the ABC commentary about it out there. But if you actually look at the evidence and if you actually look at the conduct of the police and if you actually look at the conduct of the DPP, those who are serious about the wellbeing of victims and bona fide complainants would be saying, come on, we need better from the Victorian police on this. We need better from the DPP than this. And we definitely deserve better from the Chief Justice and the President of the Court of Appeal of Victoria, otherwise what we get is years of this sort of trauma in the community generally. To say nothing of someone like Pell being put in jail for 404 days where he's in lockdown, in solitary confinement for 23 hours a day on a case which clearly should never have been brought in the first case.

Kieran Gilbert: Cardinal Pell said that it was not a referendum on the Catholic Church, his case in his statement. But fundamentally, do you think that he was held responsible, given your analysis of the case and the stumbles by the various levels of the law, whether it be the police or the DPP? Given your view on that, do you think that he was held basically accountable, being the most senior Catholic in the country for the other sins of the Catholic Church in this case?

Frank Brennan: That's a possibility. Kieran, but I don't know, none of us knows because we're not in the minds of the jury. See, the way the criminal justice system works is the High Court of Australia quite properly, unanimously has said that no rational jury could have been convinced beyond reasonable doubt that what was alleged actually occurred. Now, that conclusion should have been simply reached by all three judges of the Court of Appeal of Victoria. Now, what led the jury into such error in this particular case? We don't know.

My own hunch and it's only a hunch, but I sat there during some of the first and second trials. My hunch was, I think it was the second trial, was two weeks after Prime Minister Morrison had given his speech in the parliament, where he made the National Apology to those who were victims. And he said, we believe you. So I think that was there in the mind of the jury. Well, what does it mean to say, we believe you, other than to convict regardless of whatever conflicts there might be in evidence?

Frank Brennan: I think that was a factor. My own hunch has always been that a big factor was that Pell himself did not give evidence. And I suspect that a lot of the jurors sat there looking at a defence barrister like Richter who had a fearsome reputation, cross-examining the complainant, I think for over a day. But then Pell just sitting there silent. And I suspect that some of the jurors thought: we're sick of the Catholic Church having money available to employ flash lawyers and they then just sit there silent. Now, that's only speculation on my part, but that was the hunch that I had as I sat through some of the proceedings.

Kieran Gilbert: Now, as you've said and you've written that you think that this was an avoidable trauma for witness J as well in this matter –

Frank Brennan: Absolutely. What he's been put through has been hell.

Kieran Gilbert: Sure. Yeah. well, you know, you reflect on that for our viewers. And also in the context of the, you know, the countless other victims who I guess I mean, I was at the appeals court, I saw outside the Supreme Court of Victoria the tears from many survivors who had a lot invested in this case.

Frank Brennan: Sure. Yeah. For them, it was emblematic. But let's, I mean, let's think about the complainant, Mr. J. I mean, I wasn't at the committal proceedings, but we've got the book by Lucie Morris-Marr. And she says that the evidence that was given at the committal was that I think it was back in 2014 that this boy's mother, or I suppose he was a young man by then, that the mother had contacted an organisation called Broken Rites and reported she was worried about her son because he'd been abused by a Parish Priest in a Parish somewhere else some years before. And then it was six months later that the mother made contact again to make mention about St. Patrick's Cathedral. And then the name Pell came up.

Now, when you've got a situation like that, it does require very critical and sensitive Victorian police work. I give full marks to the Victorian police for accompanying victims and complainants on their journeys on these things. But where I'm very critical of them is that I think they have done a great disservice to this complainant because basically they then disengaged in doing just the ordinary detective work. If I could give one example, Kieran, when the police flew to Rome with the deputy commissioner of police, Shane Patton, and he's got his name in the ring there to replace Mr Ashton when he goes later in the year. So this is very deep in the Victorian police force, their commitment to this case. When they got to Rome, they had put to Pell that the procession that took place after mass was basically an internal procession where the boys were just walking along the corridor near the sacristy and then they went and started poking around. Now, that would have made some sense. It was Pell who pointed out and said, well, hang on. No, we didn't do that. We used to have an external procession, a long procession right around the Cathedral. And so when they went back to Australia, they presumably did some detective work about that, but not very much. So it wasn't till the committal proceeding that Richter actually asked the complainant about how it was that he travelled into the sacristy, where he then described a very elaborate route, which, guess what, would have taken five minutes from the end of mass for the boys to get him to the sacristy. Well, the case had been built on the basis that there was five or six minutes in which this could have happened. Well, five minutes had disappeared.

Now, that sort of basic police work, you know, you don't have to be much more than Inspector Clouseau to do the work on that. And to go back to a complainant and say, hang on there are basic things, it's not that we don't believe you, but there are basic things here about your story which don't add up and we've got to get it better. That was never done.

Kieran Gilbert: Cardinal Pell is a polarising figure. And –

Frank Brennan: He certainly is, I've had my fights with him for years.

Kieran Gilbert: I know you have. But if you like him or you detest the individual concerned. How do you reflect on that –

Frank Brennan: That's precisely – the way I reflect on that – that's what the rule of law is about, Kieran. It's about living in a country where you can proudly say it doesn't matter whether you are Cardinal Pell, it doesn't matter whether you're an Aboriginal person out of sorts, out back of Bourke, whoever you are, that you get justice according to law. And we have breached that principle very fundamentally in this case until we got to the High Court of Australia. And so, I say all praise to the highest court in the land. And I think the behaviour of the senior judiciary, of the Director of Public Prosecutions and of the Deputy Police Commissioner in Victoria, I think it's been absolutely below par. And I think it has meant that the rule of law has not been extended without fear or favour. And that's why someone like myself - sure, I've had all sorts of fights with Cardinal Pell in the past and I'll probably have some more in the future. They'll be about esoteric theological points in the Catholic Church which won't need to worry your viewers. But I couldn't care whether I like him or dislike him, whether his theology is the same as mine or not.

If a prominent citizen like that is going to be targeted by the police, by the DPP, and then given second rate treatment by an appeal court, I say I've got a job to do to be out there and say the rule of law should apply to everyone, including one George Pell, even though he's a cardinal of the Catholic Church.

Kieran Gilbert: And finally, there is a call now for the Attorney General, it's a separate issue, it's not in relation to this matter. It's a separate matter. Going back to when he was a priest in Ballarat in the 70s and 80s about the Royal Commission, a lot of it was redacted. Do you think that that should be released now in terms of the references to Cardinal Pell?

Frank Brennan: I think in principle, everything in a Royal Commission report should be unredacted as soon as all criminal processes have been played through. Now, in relation to Pell, I would say this. Given the abysmal behaviour of the Director of Public Prosecutions in relation to Pell in particular, given that she did not follow her own protocol in the way she conducted herself in the High Court. I would say this. That if there is to be a suggestion that Pell be prosecuted again for an offence, no matter how historical or whatever, three points to make.

First, it not be the police, but the DPP, that discharge that function. We had too much Mickey Mouse stuff going on with this case in the first instance, with the police going ahead and saying that he'd be charged and it was just a media farce. That's got to be the job of the DPP. Second, the DPP should be required to show that they apply the principles of their protocol. And thirdly, I would say in this particular instance that the DPP should have the humility to accept, given her demonstrable failures in this case, that it is essential if there be consideration of the prosecution of Pell of any other historic offence, that the brief simply be handed to a reputable retired judge or a reputable QC at the private bar, not part of the coterie of the DPP to give you a learned opinion, whether, according to the DPP's own protocol, whether or not a prosecution is warranted, that prosecution should then proceed.

But then if, as I suspect, there would be no basis for any further prosecutions, then once that's done and dusted, yes, everything in the Royal Commission report should be unredacted. And anything there that's adverse to Pell, let's see it. Anything adverse to anybody else. What we want out of that Royal Commission is transparency and justice for everyone. And that's what our Catholic Church has needed. We needed a Royal Commission to be able to do it, but to have the fruit of the

Royal Commission being messed up, and the lives of complainants being destroyed, because the police in Victoria have not done their job. I just think we've got to call a stop to that once and for all.

Kieran Gilbert: Father Frank Brennan, I appreciate your time, as always. Thank you.

8

Homily for Wednesday of Holy Week

8 April 2020

Today, the Wednesday of Holy Week on the cusp of our Easter Triduum, we hear the words of the prophet Isaiah, Chapter 50:

Does anyone start proceedings

against me?

Then let us go to court together.

Who thinks he has a case against me?

Let him approach me.

Yesterday the nation witnessed a huge court case bringing to conclusion the trial of Cardinal George Pell. The court decision has triggered many reactions around the country, despite our physical distancing and isolation. There are many voices out there - if not in the streets, then on the airwaves. Let's be attentive to the voices of those most involved in these court proceedings.

None of us knows the identity of the complainant, nor should we. We know him only as Mr J. Yesterday he issued a statement through his lawyer saying:

'My journey has been long and I am relieved that it is over. I have my ups and downs. The darkness is never far away. Despite the stress of the legal process and public controversy I have tried hard to keep myself together. I am OK. I hope that everyone who has followed this case is OK.'

Isaiah says:

So that I may know how to reply to the wearied

he provides me with speech.

Each morning he wakes me to hear,

to listen like a disciple.

The Lord Yahweh has opened my ear.

Whatever our view about the court decision, let's open our ears to hear Mr J and all those who have suffered dreadful trauma in their lives. Let's use our power of speech to learn how we might reply to those who are weary, those for whom darkness is never far away, those having their ups and downs trying to keep themselves together.

The other key person in the court proceedings is Cardinal George Pell who now walks free after 400 days in prison, most often solitary confinement. He too has issued a statement:

'I hold no ill will toward my accuser, I do not want my acquittal to add to the hurt and bitterness so many feel; there is certainly hurt and bitterness enough. The only basis for long term healing is truth and the only basis for justice is truth, because justice means truth for all.'

Isaiah says:

For my part, I made no resistance

neither did I turn away.

I offered my back to those who struck me,

my cheeks to those who tore at my beard;

I did not cover my face

against insult and spittle.

The Lord Yahweh comes to my help,

so that I am untouched by the insults.

Whatever the graffiti on cathedral walls and whatever the demonstrations outside the Carmelite monastery, let's not bear ill will towards each other, let's not allow this latest court ruling to add to the bitterness and hurt which so many are feeling at this time.

Let's pray for Mr J and Cardinal Pell this Easter that they might be assured that justice, truth and healing are near at hand. Let's speak truth to power. Let's enact justice where there is oppression. Let's be attentive to the tender moments of healing even in the midst of controversy and division. Let's make our way to the passion, death and resurrection of the Lord.

9

The Cardinal Pell case highlights the serious need for legal reform[6]

The Tablet

11 April 2020

Cardinal George Pell has been acquitted of all charges of child sexual abuse by Australia's highest court - the High Court of Australia. The High Court is similar to the Supreme Courts in the UK and USA. The court has seven judges. In criminal cases, they usually sit only a bench of five judges. In Pell's case, the full bench of seven sat. They knew the world was watching. They often write separate opinions. But in the case of Cardinal Pell they all put their name to one judgment. They unanimously upheld his appeal and in almost record time.

At the appeal, the Director of Public Prosecutions (DPP) for the State of Victoria where Pell was charged appeared in person. She submitted to the court that if the judges were minded to uphold the appeal, they should at least refer the matter back to the Victorian state court for final determination. All seven High Court judges described that submission with one word: 'specious'. This highlights why the Pell trial needs some local context to be readily understood by overseas readers.

---

6   Available at https://tinyurl.com/2yzceubz

English readers are used to jokes about kangaroo courts in the land down under. But in this instance, overseas readers need to understand that all is not well with the system of criminal justice in the Australian state of Victoria. Cardinal Pell has been a major casualty in this clash and decline of institutions. The unsuspecting complainant who brought the case against him has had to suffer untold additional trauma because of the shortcomings of the Victoria Police and the office of Public Prosecutions.

Some background is needed. In Victoria, there is a long running royal commission investigating how the Victoria Police came to enlist a defence barrister as a human source to inform on her own clients. In the area of criminal justice, the abuse of process does not get much worse. It's estimated that this gross abuse by the Victoria police brings into question about 1300 convictions, including some of the most awful criminals in the state. One of the key persons with involvement in this perverse police operation was Graham Ashton who is now the Victorian police commissioner.

The Victoria Police went to great lengths to disguise this operation. In an earlier case in the High Court of Australia, Commissioner Ashton suggested that the defence barrister had been signed up as a human source only in 2005, and that this extraordinary step had been taken to counter the emergency of dealing with gang warfare killings on the streets of Melbourne. However, other evidence submitted to the Royal Commission revealed that, in fact, she had been signed up as a police informer long before that. At the royal commission, the DPP rightly submitted: 'The Chief Commissioner made no attempt to correct the record of facts before the High Court so as to make clear to the Court that (the human source) had, in fact, been formally registered prior to 2005; even though the fact of that earlier registration would have contradicted the Chief Commissioner's submission in that Court that (she) had become a registered police informer only because of 'assurances' made to her in 2002 and 2003.'

When the media got onto this, they reported: 'Victoria's Director of Public Prosecutions has accused senior police, including Chief Commissioner Graham Ashton, of misleading the High Court and the Supreme Court of Victoria about the full history of its relationship with (the) barrister-turned-informer'. Curiously the DPP then issued a press release saying: 'At no time did I accuse senior police, including Chief Commissioner Graham Ashton, of misleading the High Court and Supreme Court. Both myself and the Office of Public Prosecutions continue to enjoy a strong and close working relationship with Victoria Police.' This demonstrates what a complex web there is in Victoria between the police and the DPP.

It's important that international readers also appreciate that when George Pell became archbishop of Melbourne in 1996, he took immediate steps to set up the 'Melbourne Response' with a series of expert panels to deal with issues of child sexual abuse in the church. Between 1996 and 2012, the church and the Victoria police worked closely together on protocols dealing with this vexed issue. The church's commissioner, the late Peter O'Callaghan QC, worked closely with high ranking state and police officials to ensure that the Melbourne Response complied with all state requirements. In April 2012, the Victorian Parliament set up a parliamentary inquiry into the handling of child abuse by religious and other non-government organisations. It found that 'there was no indication at any time before April 2012 Victoria Police told the Catholic Archdiocese of Melbourne that it had any concerns about the Melbourne response'. In October 2012, Mr Ashton appeared before the committee and expressed serious concerns about the Church's mode of dealing with abuse allegations. He was less than honest. The parliamentary committee reported: 'It is clear that Victoria Police paid inadequate attention to the fundamental problems of the Melbourne Response arrangements until relatively recently in April 2012 and that, when they did become the subject of public attention, Victoria Police representatives endeavoured quite unfairly to distance the organisation from them.'

From then on, the Victoria Police set out to get Pell, and they did. Some Australians, including many victims of child sexual abuse, revile George Pell. Others hold him in high esteem. This week's High

Court decision is unlikely to change personal views of the man, but this judgment concerns the administration of the criminal justice system in the state of Victoria as it impacts on everyone, both accused and victims, who deserve justice according to law.

The Pell saga has now run for over four years, ever since the Victoria Police commenced an operation on Christmas Eve 2015 seeking evidence of any wrongdoing by Pell around his cathedral during the years 1996-2001 when he was archbishop of Melbourne. This extraordinary trawling exercise turned up only one complainant whose allegations were taken all the way to trial. The complainant gave evidence that he and his now deceased companion were sexually assaulted by Pell in the priests' sacristy at the cathedral immediately after solemn Sunday mass in St Patrick's Cathedral in late 1996. He also gave evidence that Pell assaulted him in the sacristy corridor after another mass a couple of months later. These are the five charges that the High Court threw out this week. Thus, the anger and relief at the decision.

The Australian High Court has spoken definitively, unanimously and with one voice. The seven Justices have agreed that in relation to all five charges, 'there is a significant possibility that an innocent person has been convicted'. The court ordered that Pell's 'convictions be quashed and judgments of acquittal be entered in their place'. Pell is now home with the Carmelite sisters in Melbourne able to celebrate mass at Easter. The complainant, having undergone extensive periods of stress, is left to get on with his life as best he can, wondering what was the point of this protracted legal trauma. He is the hapless victim in this showdown between institutions.

The court accepted that the jury had assessed the complainant's evidence 'as thoroughly credible and reliable'. In the Victorian Court of Appeal, that step was enough for two of the judges to uphold the convictions. But the dissenting judge, Mark Weinberg, Australia's most experienced criminal appeal court judge, thought that was only the first step of a court's inquiry, and not the last. All seven High Court judges agreed. The court needed to examine the record of all the evidence in the case 'to see whether, notwithstanding that assessment, the court is satisfied that the jury, acting rationally, ought nonetheless to have entertained a reasonable doubt as to proof of guilt'. The court unanimously decided that any jury acting rationally must have had a reasonable doubt.

In addition to the complainant, there were many other witnesses called by the prosecution in Pell's case. They included 23 witnesses 'who were involved in the conduct of solemn Mass at the Cathedral or who were members of the choir in 1996 and/or 1997'. Many of these witnesses were also thoroughly credible and reliable, though their reliability faltered at times given that they were trying to recall what they would have been doing after mass in St Patrick's Cathedral on a particular Sunday 22 years before. The honesty of these witnesses was not questioned by the prosecution.

The High Court found that many of these witnesses had given consistent evidence that placed Pell on the steps of the Cathedral for at least 10 minutes after mass on 15 and 22 December 1996, the only possible dates when the first four offences could have been committed. The prosecution 'conceded that the offences alleged in the first incident could not have been committed if, following Mass, (Pell) had stood on the Cathedral steps greeting congregants for ten minutes.'

The court also found that there was unquestioned evidence by honest witnesses that placed Pell in company with his Master of Ceremonies when he returned to the priests' sacristy to disrobe. Furthermore, there was abundant evidence of 'continuous traffic into and out of the priests' sacristy for ten to 15 minutes' after the altar servers returned to the sacristy at the end of the procession at the conclusion of mass. There was no 5-6 minute hiatus for the offences to occur with Pell, the complainant and his companion in the sacristy alone, together and uninterrupted, straight after mass.

The tragedy of this case for everyone, and especially for the complainant, is that a police investigation is expected to identify problems with a complainant's account. In this case it did not.

When interviewed in Rome back in October 2016 by Victorian police officers who were being supervised by their Deputy Commissioner Shane Patton, Pell told the police that the sacristy was 'a hive of activity' after mass with altar servers, sacristan, assistant sacristan, money collectors and any concelebrating priests coming and going. He said he would have been accompanied at all relevant times by his MC Charles Portelli. Incidentally, Patton has now put his hat in the ring as Ashton's successor when the commissioner position becomes vacant later this year.

The police returned to Australia and interviewed Portelli and the sacristan Max Potter who basically confirmed all that Pell had said about the 'hive of activity'. But the police did not bother to interview one single altar server. They made no inquiries about money collectors or concelebrating priests. They proceeded to charge Pell - with great media fanfare. They went ahead building a case on the basis that the priests' sacristy might have been left vacant and open on this one particular day – contrary to all church routine and ritual. Yet the High Court rightly observed that 'adherence to ritual and compliance with established liturgical practice is a defining feature of religious observance.'

The farce of the case was the belated attempt by the Director of Public Prosecutions to create the space for the necessary 5-6 minute hiatus. At trial, the prosecutor had suggested, contrary to the evidence, that the altar servers might have adjourned to another room, for no reason, for 5-6 minutes before being called back to the priests' sacristy to resume their duties at the end of mass. He had to withdraw that suggestion before the jury. In the High Court, the DPP submitted once again that the servers might have adjourned to another room or to the sanctuary to assist the sacristan. The High Court dealt with this suggestion kindly but firmly: 'The submission comes close to repeating the submission which the prosecutor withdrew at the trial. There was no evidence that the altar servers went to their room to disrobe prior to returning to the sanctuary in order to assist in clearing away the sacred vessels and other objects.'

In the end, there was just not the evidence to support the complainant's account. There never was. For the good of all victims and complainants, the Victorian Police and DPP need to review their procedures in cases like this. Those who neither canonise nor despise George Pell should be grateful that the High Court of Australia has finally delivered justice according to law in this protracted Victorian saga.

We all need to spare a thought for the complainant in these proceedings. There can be no doubt that he has suffered serious trauma in his life. I am sorry for the added trauma he has now suffered through the processes of the law. Much of it was avoidable. These processes have also re-traumatised many other people who have experienced institutional child sexual abuse and who have placed hope in our legal system. Their situation would have been assisted if the police in this case had undertaken competent, objective policing. The DPP could have helped by complying with its own published policy that it 'not put forward theories that are not supported by evidence'. These failures in due process caused needless pain and avoidable harm to Mr J, Cardinal Pell and the community. Meanwhile, the Victorian criminal justice system cries out for reform.

10

Pell's Sad Saga of Suffering[7]

The Weekend Australian,

11-12 April 2020

Two weeks before Cardinal George Pell faced the jury of his 12 fellow citizens who convicted him of vile sexual assaults on two choir boys, Prime Minister Scott Morrison delivered the national apology to victims of child sexual assault. Morrison told Parliament: 'Not just as a father, but as a prime minister, I am angry too at the calculating destruction of lives and the abuse of trust, including those who have abused the shield of faith and religion to hide their crimes, a shield that is supposed to protect the innocent, not the guilty. They stand condemned ... On behalf of the Australian people, this parliament and our government ... I simply say I believe you, we believe you, your country believes you.'

In Pell's case, the jury believed the complainant Mr J who said he recalled events from 22 years previously when he was a 13-year-old member of the St Patrick's Cathedral choir. They were convinced beyond reasonable doubt that Pell committed these crimes in the priests' sacristy after a Sunday 11am solemn mass. Now the High Court has unanimously decided that the jury got it wrong. The court has ruled that on the evidence presented at trial, no jury could properly be convinced beyond reasonable doubt that these assaults occurred. The highest court in the land has determined that Cardinal

---

7   Available at https://tinyurl.com/sfcff2uc

Pell is not guilty of these charges.

How can this be? What lessons are to be learnt for the well-being of victims and complainants? How can the Victorian criminal justice system be improved to assist complainants who come forward many years after experiencing dreadful trauma, at the same time protecting those who are wrongly accused?

The problem with the Pell case from the start was the way in which it was handled by the police. For some months, the Office of the Director of Public Prosecutions tried to get the police to improve the brief of evidence. The police then decided to go it alone and charge Pell on summons. With a lack of due diligence, the police failed to interview possible key witnesses. The police told the media, 'Advice was received and sought from the office of public prosecutions, however ultimately, the choice to charge Cardinal Pell was one that was made by Victoria police.' John Champion, who was DPP at the time, said that his office would   conduct the criminal proceedings. From then on, the office of the DPP went to extraordinary lengths trying to cobble together a case. This was the second problem. Once the trial process commenced, the DPP kept shifting ground all the way up to the High Court, promoting a case inconsistent with the evidence.

What does it mean for society to believe Mr J in the way the Prime Minister indicated? It should mean that when J presents a complaint to police, he is treated respectfully and sensitively, while he pieces together his traumatic memories of past assaults. The police did this, and they did it well. Commendably, the Victoria Police have worked closely with victims' groups and their lawyers. While police were listening respectfully to J, they should still have been committed to orthodox investigation, collecting evidence consistent with J's account and scrutinising any evidence inconsistent with his account. The police should then have gone back to J pointing out how his honest recollection of past events did not tally with the evidence of routine practices in the cathedral – evidence which could have been provided to the police by perfectly decent, honest people doing their best to recall what they routinely did in a highly organised liturgical setting over twenty years before. A solemn mass with an archbishop in attendance in St Patrick's Cathedral is a bit like a military parade when it comes to discipline and ritual. The police did not even make the most rudimentary inquiries of those who knew, like the back of their hands, the procedures for a solemn mass.

J alleged that he and his friend R were assaulted for 5-6 minutes by Pell after mass in the priests' sacristy (the 'sacristy') when the sacristy door was unlocked and open, and when there were no other persons in the room. It's important to note that there are three sacristies in the cathedral: the archbishop's sacristy, the priests' sacristy, and the workers' sacristy which is also called the utility room. The DPP told the High Court that Pell 'would ordinarily have used the Archbishop's Sacristy to robe and disrobe'. But Pell did not ordinarily use the archbishop's sacristy prior to 1997. In fact, there was no evidence that Pell had ever used the archbishop's sacristy for disrobing before 1997. He used the priests' sacristy which was also frequented by any priests participating in a mass, as well as the altar servers when attending to sacred vessels, ferrying them back from the sanctuary. Priests don't go into the workers' sacristy where altar servers disrobe and attend to things like candles, flowers and incense. The startling gap in the police investigation was their failure to interview altar servers and other key people who were routinely in the priests' sacristy.

J also alleged a second attack by Pell a couple of months later in a corridor of the cathedral when there would have been 40 or 50 people standing around and when Pell would have been standing beside Fr Brendan Egan who had just said the mass. J never mentioned the later assault to his friend R. I won't complicate the story by saying anything further about that assault as Sergeant Christopher Reed, the lead investigator, admitted that neither he nor any other police undertook any investigation of this allegation, and for whatever reason, they never even spoke to Egan, who though no longer a priest lives and works in Melbourne.

Police Operations

J provided the police with 2 statements in June and July 2015. Over a year later, the police then interviewed Pell in Rome on 20 October 2016.

In the Rome interview Pell was told for the first time that the main allegations related to an incident immediately after mass in the cathedral. Prior to then, Pell thought the police inquiries related to an incident after choir practice. Apart from expressing his incredulity about J's allegations, Pell went to great lengths in the interview to explain how it was just not possible for him to be alone in the priests' sacristy with 2 choir boys immediately after mass.

He told the police how he would always be accompanied by his MC Monsignor Charles Portelli while robed. He would stop at the front door after mass and greet parishioners. The priests' sacristy after mass would be 'a hive of activity' with altar servers coming and going, ferrying sacred vessels used during mass from the sanctuary to the sacristy. Any priests who had celebrated the mass with Pell would be in the sacristy disrobing, and the collectors would be bringing in the money from the collections.

The police followed up by interviewing Portelli on 6 December 2016. Portelli later gave evidence in court consistent with Pell's account to the police about the busy state of the sacristy after mass, and about the cast of characters who would have been coming and going in the sacristy at that time.

The police then had 1 year and 8 months to review what Pell and Portelli had separately told them. They did not interview one single altar server. They did not interview one single concelebrating priest other than Portelli who had confirmed Pell's account. They did not interview one single money collector. They charged Pell instead.

Pell faced a first trial before a jury which could not agree in late August 2018. During that trial, the defence asked the DPP to include an altar server as a witness. This server Jeff Connor had kept a diary.

With that diary it was possible to establish that the only possible dates for the main incident were 15 December 1996 and 22 December 1996. Connor's diary also contained names of other altar servers from that time. After Connor had given his evidence about his diary, the defence was then able to ask him about the usual practice of altar servers entering the sacristy after mass.

At the end of mass, some servers would lead the procession out of the cathedral. They would be followed by about 60 choristers. Then would come any concelebrating priests followed by Portelli and Pell accompanied by a couple of other servers who would take charge of Pell's mitre and crozier should he want to put them aside. For example, if staying on the front steps to greet parishioners for any length of time, Pell would hand over the crozier and mitre. According to J, Pell arrived at the sacristy without his mitre and crozier. The crozier, symbolic of the shepherd's staff, is a sacred and valuable piece of liturgical equipment. It would not be left lying around. If Pell did not bring it with him, the crozier bearer or sacristan would have brought it back to the sacristy before Pell arrived (if Pell stayed on the steps greeting parishioners), or with Pell (if Pell handed it over at the end of the procession), or shortly after Pell arrived in the sacristy. And the mitre would be returned by the mitre bearer.

Having reached the front door of the cathedral, the procession took an external route on the day of the alleged incident. The route from the sanctuary to the front west door and then externally to the priests' sacristy was 300 steps, taking about 4 minutes. J told the jury that he and his friend cut from the procession late in the piece, backtracked and took another route through the south transept to the priests' sacristy. Their route was about 400 steps. It would have taken them about 5 minutes to reach the priests' sacristy if they had gone straight there. But J told the jury that he and R 'were sort of poking around in the corridors' before they got there.

J and R would have reached the priests' sacristy more than a minute *after* the first group of altar servers entered. On entry, the altar servers bowed to the cross and set about ferrying sacred vessels from the sanctuary to the sacristy. The sanctuary is just 50 steps from the sacristy. Any concelebrating priests would have been disrobing.

At the second trial, a second server Daniel McGlone had come forward of his own volition. He is now a practising barrister. He recalled serving Pell's masses at about the time of the alleged incident. He, too, was able to confirm to the jury that altar servers would come into the sacristy at the end of mass, bow to the cross, and commence their clearing duties.

The police had never in all their months of investigation seen fit to interview one single altar server. Even though they had Connor's diary for two months before the second trial started, they did not track down and interview any altar server whose name appeared in the diary. Here is the evidence of Christopher Reed, the chief police investigator being cross examined by Pell's lawyer Robert Richter:

So what happens is this; apart from the fact that we tracked down Mr Connor you had not tracked down any altar servers at all?---No, that's correct.

But the altar servers were a very, very important part of this investigation?---Well, not during the investigative stage, no, we were concerned with the choir boys specifically, because the events that have been alleged occurred surrounding the choir boys, not the altar servers that were in a different location and had a different role.

But there weren't any choir boys present when this happened, alleged to have happened?---Well, there weren't any altar servers.

There weren't any of those present - - -?---There weren't any altar servers alleged to be present either.

Alleged by J, that is.

Reed had said that the 'events that have been alleged occurred surrounding the choir boys, not the altar servers'. The contrary was true. There would never have been any additional choir boys in the sacristy. The choristers go straight to their choir room after mass to disrobe and return their sheet music. The issue was what had happened to the altar servers who would normally be in the priests' sacristy.

Herein lies the problem.

Instead of investigating the allegations, the police simply accepted J's account, including the assertion that there were no altar servers present during any of the periods that the first incident could have occurred. They interviewed no altar servers. But they interviewed over 30 choristers. Why? Because J was a chorister.

This policing technique, if applied to other cases, would compromise many a criminal investigation. Let's consider an example where police receive a report of a crime, not from a victim but from someone who is simply an honest eyewitness. Imagine if a pedestrian claimed to witness a bank robbery, telling the police that she did not see any bank tellers in attendance when the bank vault was raided. The police then spend 18 months interviewing 30 other pedestrians, but they decide not to interview any bank tellers because the pedestrian witness said she did not see any. The police would want to interview all available bank tellers if only to learn from them what their usual practices were, assisting the police to understand how the robbery could possibly have happened. The necessity of interviewing the bank tellers as part of a proper investigation is underscored if there is evidence that routinely bank tellers would be in attendance at the time the robbery occurred.

The first incident involving four sexual assaults on two boys is alleged to have occurred in a room which, at all relevant times, was either locked and inaccessible to the boys, or a hive of activity with persons constantly coming and going, including altar servers ferrying sacred vessels from the sanctuary, concelebrating priests who were disrobing, and functionaries transporting the money from the collections to safe keeping in the vault in the priests' sacristy.

The jury needed to be convinced beyond reasonable doubt that there was a period of six minutes after mass when Pell, J and R could be alone together in the priests' sacristy. That six-minute period had either to end *before* the returning altar servers bowed to the cross or to begin more than a minute *after* they bowed to the cross when J and R entered the room. It could not include the time when the altar servers bowed to the cross as that would mean that Pell, J and R would not have been together, alone and uninterrupted, for the necessary time for the offences to occur.

There could not have been any such six-minute period *before* the entry of the altar servers because J and R had not reached the priests' sacristy by then, and Pell was still at the back of the procession or on the steps talking to parishioners.

There could not have been any six-minute period *after* the entry of the altar servers because the altar servers would have needed to adjourn somewhere else after they had bowed to the cross. There was no 'somewhere else'. They would not have gone to the nearby workers' sacristy. If they had been waiting in the corridor outside the sacristies, they would have seen Pell coming and he would have seen them.

No rational jury could have been satisfied beyond reasonable doubt that there was a six minute window available for the offences to have occurred in the priests' sacristy after solemn 11am mass on a Sunday.

DPP Theories

Then came the second problem.

The prosecutor went to extraordinary lengths to try and establish the necessary six minute 'hiatus' in an empty sacristy. The prosecutor tried to separate Pell and Portelli so as to get Pell into the room alone with the boys. The prosecutor then went to even greater lengths trying to prove that the altar servers were out of the room, having deftly airbrushed the money collectors and any concelebrating priests out of the picture completely.

The prosecutor and the DPP had five speculative theories. And they all collapsed in a heap. Portelli admitted to being a smoker. In the first trial, the prosecutor Mark Gibson QC suggested that Portelli might have been desperate for a smoke after mass, and that he might have skipped off somewhere fully robed for a quick draw. Portelli rejected the idea out of hand. Gibson went ahead in his final address to the jury putting the suggestion. Justice Kidd, the trial judge, rightly directed him to retract. In the second trial, Gibson gave it another go. He asked Portelli if he might have ducked out for a smoke straight after mass leaving Pell on his own. Portelli replied: 'It would be as appropriate as for instance His Honour walking down William Street dressed as he is smoking a cigarette, which is not done.' Not to be deterred Gibson once again tried the speculative theory with the jury and once again was required to retract in his final address. Corrected by the judge, Gibson told the jury that even though Portelli had denied going off for a smoke, 'I argued to you that perhaps he did. Well, that's speculating. So, that's not to be taken into account, perhaps he did. His evidence is he didn't. So I just wanted to make that clear, because it's the evidence that we base these decisions on, not speculation'.

The second theory was that Portelli might have been absent from Pell's side if only for a couple of minutes to go to the sanctuary to organise the books and sermon notes for an event Pell might have had in the cathedral later that day. But Pell had no mass scheduled later in the cathedral on either the 15 or 22 December. Gibson suggested that Pell might have been going to say the regular evening mass in the cathedral. But there was no evidence of that. The archbishop having celebrated the 11am solemn mass never says the low-key evening mass. It's said by one of the priests on the cathedral staff.

The third theory was that the altar servers having bowed to the crucifix after their 4-minute procession into the priests' sacristy might then have adjourned for a further 5-6 minutes to the workers' sacristy awaiting further instructions before returning to the priests' sacristy to resume their duties. This was contrary to all the evidence, including the evidence of the two experienced altar servers

Connor and McGlone. There was absolutely no evidence of such a proposition. The judge directed Gibson to correct the suggestion. Gibson returned after lunch and told the jury: 'Mr Foreman and members of the jury, before lunch I had spoken about there being this period of time after the altar servers had bowed to the crucifix in the priests' sacristy and before Mr Potter had started ferrying items from the sanctuary to the priests' sacristy. I think I might have said that the altar servers were in their workers' sacristy during this five to six-minute time period. There is, of course, no evidence of that, and there's no evidence of where they were. There is evidence of where they weren't from J, and that is that they weren't in the priests' sacristy, so I was inviting you to conclude that it was during this period waiting for the green light from Mr Potter that, wherever the altar servers were, it was not in the priests' sacristy.'

This theory highlighted the whole problem with the crown case.

The evidence of honest, reliable witnesses called by the crown and never contradicted was to be airbrushed out of the picture because it did not fit with the complainant's account.

The fourth and fifth speculative theories did not arise until the new DPP Kerri Judd QC appeared personally in the High Court, leading Gibson who had prosecuted the case through the committal proceedings and both trials before then participating in the appeal in the Victorian Court of Appeal.

These theories were breathtaking. They highlighted the incoherence of the crown case. When pressed by the High Court bench on where one could find these necessary 5-6 minutes when Pell could be alone with the boys in the priests' sacristy, Judd threw all caution and evidence to the wind. Judd was asked by Justice Virginia Bell: 'On the evidence, once the altar servers bowed to the crucifix, on their account where did they go?' Judd responded that there was evidence 'that they went to what they called the "worker sacristy" to unrobe. That was a different sacristy. That was the workers' room or the candle room.' When asked by the bench, 'Is this going back to the position that the prosecution disavowed at trial?', Judd threw Gibson under the bus, replying that Gibson had 'incorrectly disavowed that there was no evidence, he was very generous in that'. She then purported to find the evidence where the altar server McGlone had said that the crozier bearer and mitre bearer had arrived at the priests' sacristy, returned their items, and then adjourned to the workers' sacristy to disrobe. Justice Bell asked her: 'Do you say they went off and changed into civilian clothing before they removed the sacred vessels?' Judd replied 'Yes'.

Anyone who knows anything about a solemn mass in St Patrick's Cathedral in those days under the keen eye of Cardinal Pell knows that it would be unthinkable for altar servers to venture unrobed on to the sanctuary. This was not just a mistake about church custom. It was a clear divergence from the evidence. Judd misquoted McGlone's evidence, overlooking that McGlone distinguished the mitre bearer and the crozier bearer from the other altar servers. McGlone simply agreed that the other altar servers would bow to the crucifix at the end of the procession and 'Then they would go and follow directions as to what they should do with the various vessels'. Even if the mitre bearer and crozier bearer had adjourned to the workers' sacristy to disrobe, having completed their tasks, the *other* servers continued their allotted tasks ferrying things from the sanctuary to the priests' sacristy while still robed. There was no evidence to the contrary.

Stretching the crown case to breaking point, Judd demonstrated, ironically, that there was no evidence capable of displacing the credible evidence of those most knowledgeable about the actions of altar servers that they would have been coming and going into the room during that contentious 5-6 minutes.

Then came the DPP's fifth theory. At trial, everyone accepted the sacristan Potter's evidence that he would allow 5- 6 minutes private prayer time for parishioners before he commenced the clearing of the sanctuary. The prayer time would commence when the procession was departing the cathedral. Anxious to find the necessary 5-6 minutes for the offending to occur in the priests' sacristy *after* the two choir boys would have spent at least five minutes leaving the cathedral and making their way to the sacristy (processing, backtracking and poking around), Judd abandoned the uncontested evidence and put suggestions which would have entailed expanding the private prayer to more than 10 minutes. Judd told the court she was 'really going to go in hard on this'. She told the court: 'how long that is and when it starts is very much dependent upon how long it takes for the cathedral to be cleared'. When the Chief Justice asked her, 'Was it put to any witness that it could be more than five to six minutes?', she rightly answered, 'No'. When the Chief Justice put to her that at trial before the jury 'the prosecutor adopts the evidence of five to six minutes and goes with it', she rightly answered, 'Yes'. But that didn't stop her from propounding yet another scenario without evidence to make it good.

For J's account of an empty sacristy at the time of the offending to have been correct, nine persons (the sacristan Max Potter, the MC Charles Portelli, and 7 altar servers) would have had to deviate without explanation from their regular, scheduled, prescribed behaviour.

Potter, Portelli, and altar server Connor all gave uncontradicted evidence that they would have done nothing different from their usual routine all those years ago on the occasion of the first incident. They could not recall having done something different. In the High Court, Justice Patrick Keane observed when questioning the DPP: 'In terms of the way the case was run, it was not open to the jury to take the view that Monsignor Portelli was not there. Monsignor Portelli gives evidence of a couple of practices that exist and says, it is possible they were not followed because of the exigencies of the particular day, but he cannot recall that there was any particular exigency that caused a departure from the practice. Is not the evidence of practice, where it is honestly given, usually regarded as powerful evidence?' Judd agreed and Keane added: 'I mean, I can say I shaved last Friday, not because I actually have a specific recollection of it, but because it was a workday and I shave on workdays.'

Portelli gave uncontested evidence that he recalled each of the masses which could have been the occasion of the first incident and that he would not have deviated for a full six minutes from his practice of accompanying the robed archbishop in procession and that he had no occasion to leave the robed archbishop for even two minutes (there being no additional archbishop's event in the cathedral that afternoon requiring him to attend to the books in the sanctuary). According to J, Pell did not have his mitre and crozier when he arrived at the sacristy. Pell would have no reason to dispense with the mitre and crozier if he stayed with the procession. It was very much part of his formal liturgical regalia. There was evidence that he used hand them over if he was departing the procession, stopping on the steps to greet parishioners at the west door.

Altar servers Connor and McGlone gave evidence that in their experience altar servers would not deviate without reason from the regular, scheduled, prescribed behaviour in the priests' sacristy after mass.

Any deviation from that behaviour would have required all those nine persons (sacristan, MC, and altar servers at the front of procession and altar servers at the back of procession) to be in another place for no known reason, without any evidence (or even suggestion) of them acting in concert. If they did not act in concert, each of them would have required a direction from someone to do something different from normal practice. There was no evidence of such a direction, and no hypothetical reason offered for such a direction.

An accused must be convicted of serious criminal offences only on the evidence. The trial prosecutor and DPP in this case promoted their own speculative case theories in an effort to get around or disregard credible evidence from its own witnesses without daring to challenge the honesty of those witnesses.

When the suppression order was lifted in February 2019, I wrote in *The Australian* (28/2/19), 'I can only hope and pray that the complainant can find some peace, able to get on with his life, whichever way the appeal goes...Should the appeal succeed, the Victoria Police should review the adequacy of the investigation of these serious criminal charges.' In light of the DPP's approach at trial and in the High Court, I would also urge a review of the DPP's application of its prosecutorial discretion. This case should never have come to court.

With improved procedures by the police and the prosecution authorities, allegations made by complainants of historic sexual abuse might be accepted respectfully, with the complaints being investigated diligently and with the utmost seriousness. However, it is a disservice to complainants to treat what they say as necessarily correct. Their claims need to be tested against the evidence of other honest witnesses. It would cause less pain to everyone if these claims be tested sooner and out of the public gaze – by the police and the prosecution authorities who are able to sift out claims which would be unsustainable under light of day.

The High Court's decision should confirm, rather than undermine, belief in the jury system. Justice Mark Weinberg said during argument in the Victorian Court of Appeal, 'Juries almost always get it right, but the word is "almost".' Everyone, including victims, should be grateful to Justice Weinberg who dissented in the Court of Appeal, keeping alive the prospect that the full High Court Bench might put right the miscarriage of justice in this case.

Anne Ferguson, Chief Justice of Victoria, Chris Maxwell, President of the Court of Appeal of Victoria, and Kerri Judd, the Victorian DPP all made serious errors in the conduct of the Pell proceedings. The police investigation was badly flawed, having been supervised by the Victorian Deputy Police Commissioner Shane Patton who was in Rome with the lead investigator Christopher Reed. It took the High Court to put right this series of failures by some of Victoria's most senior officials.

There can be no doubt that Mr J has suffered serious trauma in his life. I am sorry for the added trauma he has now suffered through the processes of the law. Much of it was avoidable. These processes have also re-traumatised many other people who have experienced institutional child sexual abuse and who have placed hope in our legal system. Their situation would have been assisted if the police in this case had undertaken competent, objective policing. The DPP could have helped by complying with its own published policy that it 'not put forward theories that are not supported by evidence'. These failures in due process caused needless pain and avoidable harm to Mr J, Cardinal Pell and the community.

THREE DIFFERENT ROUTES

The witness known as 'J' gave three different versions of the route taken by himself and the other choir member following the Mass at which he claimed both had been abused.

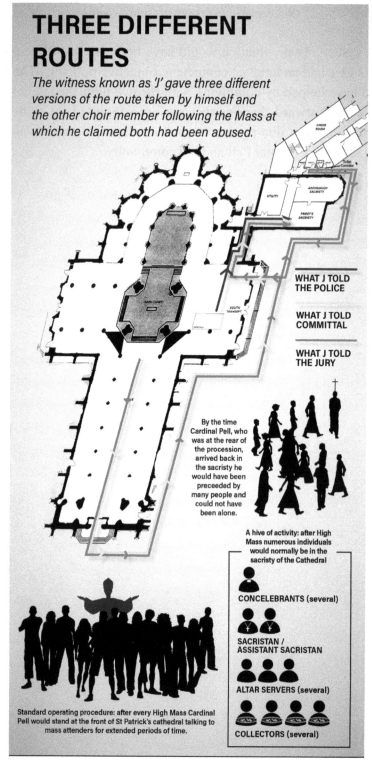

WHAT J TOLD THE POLICE

WHAT J TOLD COMMITTAL

WHAT J TOLD THE JURY

By the time Cardinal Pell, who was at the rear of the procession, arrived back in the sacristy he would have been preceeded by many people and could not have been alone.

A hive of activity: after High Mass numerous individuals would normally be in the sacristy of the Cathedral

CONCELEBRANTS (several)

SACRISTAN / ASSISTANT SACRISTAN

ALTAR SERVERS (several)

COLLECTORS (several)

Standard operating procedure: after every High Mass Cardinal Pell would stand at the front of St Patrick's cathedral talking to mass attenders for extended periods of time.

11

The Acquittal of an Innocent Man Was No Mere Technicality[8]

Altar Servers Route

Sanctuary to West Door	83 steps	1' 20"
West Door to Toilet Corridor	203 steps	2' 49"
Toilet Corridor to Priests' Sacristy Direct	22 steps	16"
TOTAL	308 steps	4' 25"

J&R Route as described at trial and put by DPP at the appeals

Sanctuary to West Door	83 steps	1' 20"
West Door to Toilet Corridor	203 steps	2' 49"
Toilet Corridor to Priests' Sacristy with Backtrack through South Transept	122 steps	1' 17"
TOTAL	408 steps	5' 26"

---

8   I circulated these remarks to some lawyers and commentators after a couple of legal academics wrote: 'Careful analysis of the full reasoning of the High Court is required to fully assess it. But, for now, this extraordinary outcome is strange justice indeed. Pell has won today on a legal technicality'. See https://theconversation.com/how-george-pell-won-in-the-high-court-on-a-legal-technicality-133156.

The legislature has specified that an appeal against conviction must be allowed 'if the appellant satisfies the court that the ... verdict of the jury is unreasonable or cannot be supported having regard to the evidence'.[9]

The High Court has previously said that 'where the evidence lacks credibility for reasons which are not explained by the manner in which it was given, a reasonable doubt experienced by the court is a doubt which a reasonable jury ought to have experienced'.[10] The question is 'whether the jury *must*, as distinct from *might*, have entertained a doubt about the appellant's guilt'.[11] In *Pell v Queen*, the High Court, following its earlier precedents, unanimously found that the jury must have entertained a doubt about Pell's guilt.

In his charge to the jury, Justice Kidd observed: 'It does seem common ground, however, between the parties, that there are some differences in [J's] accounts... In relation to the first episode concerning the priests' sacristy, at the committal Mr J drew a diagram on the cathedral plan showing the way he left the procession and veered off at the south transept into the doors. ...[T]here is that line which shows veering off from the procession, not far from the south transept and into the south transept. At trial he said they went up to the toilet corridors near the iron gate and doubled back, so that is a difference. It seems common ground there is a difference there and both parties made arguments to you about what flows from that'.

On the later version given at trial and put by the prosecution to the jury as the true account, J and R would have taken about 408 steps from the sanctuary to the west door, then processing externally to 'the toilet corridors near the iron gate', then doubling back through the south transept and into the priest's sacristy. This would have taken them about 5.5 minutes, in addition to which there would have been the time they took to be poking around. Meanwhile the altar servers who were ahead of them in the procession would have arrived at the priest's sacristy at least a minute before them, as they, having gone

---

9   *Criminal Procedure Act 2009* s 276(1)(a)

10   *M* (1994) 181 CLR 487, 494.

11   *Libke* v *The Queen*, Hayne J (with whom Gleeson CJ and Heydon J agreed), (2007) 230 CLR 559, 596-7.

directly to the priest's sacristy without backtracking to the south transept, would have taken 100 fewer steps than J and R. The servers would not have been delayed with any poking around. There is no way that J and R could have reached the priests' sacristy before the altar servers at the head of the procession.

All seven High Court judges observed in their judgment that the DPP 'maintained that the assaults occurred after the altar servers had entered the priests' sacristy and bowed to the crucifix'.[12] That would have been after those altar servers had left the sanctuary and walked 308 steps taking about 4.5 minutes. The DPP in the High Court sought to lengthen the private prayer time prior to the 'hive of activity' commencing in the priest's sacristy. Given that the assaults on J and R were alleged to have taken 5-6 minutes, there would have been a need for a private prayer time of about 10 minutes minimum. Presumably it would be closer to 12 minutes if you added the time taken for J and R to poke around, find wine, and swig etc prior to the commencement of the alleged assaults. No witness ever suggested any such thing. The High Court noted that the DPP's submission 'overlooked that, on Mallinson's account, circumstances including how many people were in the Cathedral would only account for the private prayer time allowed prior to the clearing of the sanctuary varying from 30 seconds to two minutes.'[13] The High Court noted that 'the evidence of witnesses, whose honesty was not in question' 'described continuous traffic into and out of the priests' sacristy for ten to 15 minutes after the altar servers completed their bows to the crucifix'[14].

There was no opportunity for assaults on J and R in the priests' sacristy in the absence of altar servers, sacristans, money collectors and concelebrants until 15-20 minutes after the lead servers left the sanctuary at the end of mass. The DPP did not present that as even just a theoretical possibility, let alone provide any evidence of same. There was none.

---

[12] *Pell* v *The Queen* [2020] HCA 12 (7 April 2020), para 116, available at http://eresources.hcourt.gov.au/showCase/2020/HCA/12
[13] Ibid.
[14] Ibid, paras 118-9.

12

Response to Melissa Davey

National Catholic Reporter[15]

9 October 2020

On 28 September 2020, the US based National Catholic Reporter *reported that Melissa Davey the author of* The Case of George Pell *had sharply rebutted commentators like me who had claimed that the complainant in the case presented 'confused' testimony. Davey was quoted saying: 'In the conversations that occurred between journalists and lawyers in the corridors of the courthouse, I never heard anyone who'd been present during the complainant's testimony say that he had performed badly. Instead, the complainant was described as "compelling" and "honest."'* [16] *I responded with a letter to the editor:*

You report that Melissa Davey sharply rebutted me for what I said about the Pell trial. Davey wrongly asserted that I did not have access to the trial transcript when I wrote my one article when the suppression order was lifted in February 2019. She fancifully claims inside knowledge from lawyers who heard the complainant give his evidence.

Last week at a launch of her book when asked, 'What did you come

---

[15] This letter to the editor published on 9 October 2020 was submitted to *The National Catholic Reporter* on 29 September 2020.

[16] Joshua McElwee, 'Up-close account of Pell's historic trial raises an uncomfortable question', *National Catholic Reporter*, 28 September 2020.

to think in the end of Pell's accuser?', she said, 'It didn't matter who I spoke to, who was there. Because obviously I had conversations with the legal teams in the hallways of the court between different hearings and things like that. They all described him [the complainant] as eloquent, articulate, honest'.[17]

It would be a breach of the law for any lawyer who was present for the testimony of the complainant to background a journalist on the performance of the complainant. There is no way any lawyer for the defence would have said any such thing. It would be completely unethical as well as illegal for any lawyer for the prosecution to do so. I am so confident of the ethics of the lawyers involved in the case on both sides as to assert that none of them told Davey that the complainant was eloquent, articulate and honest.

Davey quotes from my article of 26 February 2019 in which I spoke about 'the complainant being confused about all manner of things'. In that article, I told the reader, 'I heard some of the publicly available evidence and have read most of the transcript.'

In her sharp rebuke of me, Davey wrote that she 'found it incredible that commentary such as this was being published and broadcast long before transcripts could have been accessed at the court'. She was correct when she stated, 'It would take days... to thoroughly review transcripts for a case that ran for five weeks'. Pell's trial had concluded on 11 December 2018. I had access to the transcript for more than two months before writing my article. Davey could not access the transcript for some time after that. But that was her problem, not mine. I had many weeks to thoroughly review the transcripts.

---

17 In her book *The Case of George Pell*, Scribe Publications, 2020, Melissa Davey wrote at p.293: 'Jesuit priest and human-rights lawyer Frank Brennan, who attended a few days of the retrial, described the complainant's evidence as "confused", even though he had not seen or heard the complainant testify. By contrast, in the conversations that occurred between journalists and lawyers in the corridors of the courthouse, I never heard anyone who'd been present during the complainant's testimony say that he had performed badly. Instead, the complainant was described as "compelling" and "honest".'

Readers interested in my analysis of the incoherence of the prosecution case and the shortcomings of the police investigation can see my piece published after the High Court appeal [in *The Weekend Australian* on 10-11 April 2020[18]]. In her book, Davey addresses none of these deficiencies in the prosecution case and police investigation.

---

[18]   See Chapter 10

Observations After Release of the Unredacted Royal Commission Case Studies

13

What Was Pope Francis Up To, Meeting with Cardinal Pell?

A Background Paper for Jesuits

14 October 2020

On Monday, Pope Francis received Cardinal Pell in private audience, then publishing photos and video of same. Clearly this is a papal vindication of Pell and an indication to the world and to Catholics in Australia that the pope is convinced of the innocence of Pell.

What to say even just amongst ourselves about this?

There is no need to say anything further about the criminal prosecutions which culminated in the 7-0 victory for Pell in the High Court. But for the incompetence and animus of the Victoria Police, the DPP, and the two most senior judges of the state, Pell would have been cleared of those charges much sooner, or more likely, not charged at all. There is no way that he could have committed the offences alleged, and that is the only conclusion one can draw from any fair minded reading of the High Court decision.

Sadly, the incoherence of the prosecution case and the shortcomings of the police investigation in the Pell matter have now resulted in the gossip and conspiracy theories out of Rome unnecessarily impacting on the lives of the complainant in this case and of the many victims of child sexual abuse.

If only the police had done their job properly, if only the prosecution had refrained from inventing theories without evidence, and if only the two most senior judges in Victoria had conducted themselves with greater judicial deference to the law, victims and this complainant could have avoided being drawn into the vortex of Vatican intrigue.

If still in doubt about whether Pell could have done what was alleged in the criminal trial, simply ask yourself (given what you know of the procedures at a solemn mass in the cathedral) how a fully robed archbishop without mitre and without crozier could have had six minutes in the sacristy alone with two choirboys immediately after mass when there would be a series of up to seven altar servers (including mitre bearer carrying the mitre and crozier bearer carrying the crozier), money collectors, sacristans and concelebrants coming and going, and an MC at his side as he learnt the ropes at his first or second solemn Sunday mass in the cathedral. In the High Court, after years of thinking about possible scenarios, the DPP actually invented a false story with no evidence desperate to empty the sacristy of all other bodies. It just couldn't be done.

The journalistic accounts of the trial by Melissa Davey et al were largely written presuming (or at least desperately hoping) that the High Court would uphold the convictions.

There are now Catholics of good will wondering what the Pope was doing providing Cardinal Pell with such a public vindication given that there was not only the criminal trial. There were adverse findings against Pell by the royal commission. The Church has not provided any public response to the publication of those findings in May 2020.

Cardinal Pell issued this statement on 7 May 2020 when the findings were published:

> Cardinal Pell said he was surprised by some of the views of

the Royal Commission about his actions . These views are not supported by evidence.

He is especially surprised by the statements in the report about the earlier transfers of Gerald Ridsdale discussed by the Ballarat Diocesan Consultors in 1977 and 82.

The Consultors who gave evidence on the meetings in 1977 and 1982 either said they did not learn of Ridsdale's offending against children until much later or they had no recollection of what was discussed. None said they were made aware of Ridsdale's offending at these meetings.

The then Fr Pell left the Diocese of Ballarat and therefore his position as a consultor at the end of 1984.

As an Auxiliary Bishop in Melbourne 1987-96, Bishop Pell met with a delegation from Doveton Parish in 1989 which did not mention sexual assaults and did not ask for Searson's removal.

Appointed Archbishop of Melbourne on 16 August 1996, Archbishop Pell placed Fr Searson on administrative leave in March 1997 and removed him from the parish on 15 May 1997.

I thought it might be useful to provide the key adverse findings of the royal commission against Pell, offering a brief assessment of same.

The royal commission conducted case studies in Ballarat and Melbourne, making adverse findings in relation to Pell.

Ballarat

In the Ballarat hearings, several consultors of Bishop Mulkearns were asked about what was said at consultors meetings in the 1970s and 1980s particularly about the continued movement of Gerald Ridsdale. The commissioners came to focus on two consultors' meetings which Pell attended and at which the bishop communicated a decision about Ridsdale: 19 July 1977 and 14 September 1982.

At the consultors meeting on 19 July 1977, Bishop Mulkearns proposed that Ridsdale who was acting as administrator of Edenhope parish be confirmed as parish priest of Edenhope. The royal commission found that there had been 'talk' about Ridsdale in the parish of Apollo Bay in 1972 and in Inglewood in 1976. Pell denied having heard any such 'talk'. This was Pell's first ever consultors' meeting.

Here is the reasoning of the royal commission in relation to Pell's knowledge of Ridsdale's activities as at 19 July 1977:

> Cardinal Pell provided a variety of possibilities of what he expected may have been said at this meeting. His evidence was more emphatic as to what was not said. He gave evidence that he would be surprised if Bishop Mulkearns deceived him.
>
> We share that surprise. It does not logically follow that a bishop would deceive his appointed consultors, particularly given that it would be likely that they would find out elsewhere.
>
> Furthermore, given that Cardinal Pell would have been surprised if Bishop Mulkearns had deceived him, it is likely that he knew of Ridsdale's sexual transgressions.
>
> We are satisfied that, by this time, the consultors who had attended previous meetings, **including Father Madden and Father McInerney, had been told of Ridsdale's sexual transgressions**. It is inconceivable that these consultors did not know by this time, given the usual practice and the general knowledge in the community. [19]

So this was not a case of the bishop moving Ridsdale to another parish. It was simply a matter of confirming him as parish priest of the parish of which he was already Administrator. It should be noted that Frs Madden and McInerney each gave evidence that they

---

[19]   Ballarat Case Study, p. 61 at https://tinyurl.com/2hax2tje

did not learn of Ridsdale's proclivities until some years after this consultors meeting in 1977.

Thirteen pages later in their report, the commissioners state:

> Father Madden gave evidence that Bishop Mulkearns did not explain to him why the appointment of Ridsdale as his assistant priest was being made. Bishop Mulkearns did tell him Ridsdale had received counselling. Father Madden deduced there must have been some difficulties or problems. However, Father Madden told us he was 'very clear' that he first came to know that Ridsdale had engaged in wrongful activity with boys in 1988, when he left Horsham.
>
> It is appalling that Bishop Mulkearns, knowing of Ridsdale's history of offending, did not report to the police or adequately inform Father Madden of the risks posed by Ridsdale.[20]

The commission seems to have accepted the evidence of Fr Madden that he first came to know of Ridsdale's activities in 1988, so not in 1977. Having accepted this evidence, the commission notes how appalling it was that Bishop Mulkearns in 1988 had not told Fr Madden who did not know. And yet the very same commissioners have stated that they were satisfied that Madden knew back in 1977.

The commission's inconsistent findings in relation to Fr McInerney are even more incoherent. Having satisfied themselves that McInerney knew about Ridsdale at the consultors meeting on 19 July 1977, they go on later in their report to find:

> [Fr McInerney] was asked by counsel for the Church parties if he had any recollection of Bishop Mulkearns ever saying anything to the effect that Ridsdale had some issue with sexual behaviour or sexual abuse, and he said he did not recall him saying that. Father McInerney was asked if at any meeting while he was bishop's secretary he had 'any recollection' of Bishop Mulkearns or anyone else saying something to the effect that Ridsdale had or

---

[20]   Ibid, p. 74

might have sexually abused children, he said no. He said he was
not aware of Ridsdale's offending before Ridsdale was charged in
early 1993. [21]

So there you have it. The commissioners on the one hand thought
that Pell and other consultors must have known in 1977. But then
they accept that one of those consultors knew nothing until 1988,
and the other knew nothing until 1993.

Shoddy work by the commission to say the least. Pell supporters (of
whom there would be some in the Vatican) might see it as evidence
of animus by the commission towards Pell.

The second consultors' meeting attended by Pell in relation to
Ridsdale was on 14 September 1982. Bishop Mulkearns was
proposing to move Ridsdale from Mortlake parish to the Catholic
Enquiry Centre in Sydney.

All consultors including Pell denied that Mulkearns had told them
that Ridsdale was molesting children. However Fr Eric Bryant for
whom this was his first consultors' meeting had some recollection of
talk about 'homosexuality'.

Here are the findings of the commission:

> Cardinal Pell said that, because of Ridsdale's unusual number
> of appointments, the meeting would have discussed why he was
> being moved yet again and the bishop would have given some
> reason. Father Eric Bryant said the consultors were told 'there
> was a problem with homosexuality in the Diocese' and the bishop
> then 'referred to Ridsdale and what he'd done'. Bishop Finnigan
> did not recall that being said, and Cardinal Pell said it was entirely
> possible that that was the reason given.
>
> There is no reason not to accept the evidence of Father Bryant that
> Bishop Mulkearns said to the meeting that there was a problem
> with homosexuality in the Diocese and that this was the reason it

---

[21]   Ibid, p. 247

had become necessary to move Ridsdale from Mortlake. Father Bryant's testimony on this point was clear and straightforward, and it is not contradicted by the other witnesses who were present at the meeting.

Bishop Finnigan, the minute-taker, explained that, if the bishop had given child sexual abuse as the reason, it would not have been recorded in the minutes. That is convincing and is accepted. Bishop Finnigan was equivocal on whether he would have recorded homosexuality as the reason if that reason had been given. However, the absence of a recorded reason in the minutes is not inconsistent with the evidence that the bishop gave at least homosexuality as a reason and that he may have gone further and mentioned the problem as being one in relation to children.

We are satisfied Bishop Mulkearns gave reasons for it being necessary to move Ridsdale. We are satisfied that he referred to homosexuality at the meeting in the context of giving reasons for Ridsdale's move. However, we are not satisfied that Bishop Mulkearns left the explanation there.

As Cardinal Pell said, there would have been a discussion.

We are satisfied that the belief was that the appointment to the Catholic Enquiry Centre would reduce Ridsdale's access to children, whereas access to children was freely available in a parish. As Bishop Mulkearns acknowledged in his 1989 letter, the centre was 'specifically chosen to ensure he had no contact with ordinary parish work'.

Cardinal Pell gave evidence that the bishop did not give the true reason for moving Ridsdale – namely, his sexual activity with children – and that the bishop lied in not giving the true reason to the consultors.

We do not accept that Bishop Mulkearns lied to his consultors. Monsignor Fiscalini, Father Nolan and Father Finnigan all knew of allegations or complaints about Ridsdale's conduct with children before the meeting. They knew why it was necessary to move Ridsdale from Mortlake and take him out of the parish and Diocese to a position where access to children was restricted.

It is inconceivable in these circumstances that Bishop Mulkearns deceived his consultors by not telling them the true reason. There would be little utility in doing so. The secret was out in at least two parishes by 1978.

We are satisfied that Bishop Mulkearns' overwhelming concern was to protect his Diocese and the Church from further scandal. Limiting the information about Ridsdale to those outside of the Church was necessary to protect the reputation of the Church. That concern did not apply to insiders, and Bishop Mulkearns had no reason to think his consultors would speak publicly about the reasons for moving Ridsdale. The minutes of these meetings were not made public. We are satisfied that Bishop Mulkearns did not deceive his consultors.

We accept the evidence of Bishop Finnigan that, as minute-taker, he would not have recorded that the reason was child sexual abuse if the bishop had given that reason. We infer that this was to safeguard the discussions inside the room with the consultors. All matters discussed were not recorded, and we would not expect them to be.

We are satisfied that Bishop Mulkearns told the consultors that it was necessary to move Ridsdale from the Diocese and from parish work because of complaints that he had sexually abused children. A contrary position is not tenable[22].

Basically the commission was deciding that all the consultors were lying. They found that Mulkearns would have gone on to tell the consultors the real reason for moving Ridsdale. There was absolutely no evidence from anyone (including Mulkearns) that he gave such reasons.

---

[22]   Ibid, pp. 69-70

In relation to the Ballarat case study, I find Pell's statement of 7 May 2020 to be accurate. The royal commission's reasoning and attention to evidence is quite shoddy.

Melbourne

In the Melbourne case study, the commission focused on Fr Searson at Doveton. Pell was the auxiliary bishop to Archbishop Little and he was responsible for the region which included the parish of Doveton. To quote the commission: 'On 20 November 1989 Bishop Pell met with a delegation of staff from Holy Family School, together with Mr Lalor, the CEO chairperson for the primary staff group, and a representative of the staff union, Mr Palmer. The meeting was convened to discuss the concerns of staff about Father Searson.'[23] The staff told Pell that they had concerns about Searson's behaviour but they wanted him to be given a second chance. The only 'sexual impropriety' of Father Searson raised at the meeting was that he used the boys' toilets unnecessarily.

Here are the commission's findings on Pell's conduct:

> We are satisfied that, on the basis of the matters known to Bishop Pell on his own evidence (being the matters on the list of incidents and grievances and the 'non-specific' allegation of sexual misconduct), he ought reasonably to have concluded that action needed to be taken in relation to Father Searson.

> Counsel for Cardinal Pell submitted that the context of the meeting was important in assessing the response. They pointed to the fact that it was a matter of workplace relations, set up by the union representative to deal with the grievances of staff, and not one dealing with allegations of child sexual abuse. They submitted that it was the teachers who were dealing with Father Searson on a day-to-day basis and who instigated the meeting. For those reasons, the teachers' attitudes at the meeting were the best gauge

---

[23]   Melbourne Case Study, p. 103 at https://tinyurl.com/y4e9tbkk

of the nature and seriousness of the grievances conveyed. The fact that the teachers framed their concerns primarily for Father Searson's welfare and wanted him to be given a second chance, counsel said, 'speaks volumes'.

We accept that those matters should be taken into account and we have done so. The attitude of the teachers is a relevant consideration, but it was not the only consideration. The evidence of Mrs Stack was that the staff's reticence to suggest Father Searson be removed was because of their relationship to him as employees and the fact that they believed their jobs could be at risk.

Bishop Pell was in a senior position within the Archdiocese. He had previously been the bishop's representative for all areas of education (the Episcopal Vicar of Education) in the Ballarat diocese. The staff came as a delegation to him as an Auxiliary Bishop to complain about their employer. The sensitivities this presented should have been apparent to him. Rather, his response to Mr Palmer when the staff requested Father Searson be given a second chance ('Your evidence seems to have disappeared Mr Palmer') was dismissive.

Further, Bishop Pell was still required to exercise his independent judgment on the complaints before him. Regardless of the action the staff proposed, the incidents on the list of grievances indicated that Father Searson was obstructive and confrontational with staff. He had displayed cruelty to an animal in front of children and shown them a dead body in a coffin. There was a suggestion of sexual impropriety in that Father Searson was using the boys' toilets unnecessarily, even if he had offered an explanation for that conduct. Mr Stack

told Bishop Pell that Father Searson was mentally unwell and that something needed to be done. These matters, in combination with the prior allegation of sexual misconduct, ought to have indicated to Bishop Pell that Father Searson needed to be stood down.

It was incumbent on Bishop Pell, as an Auxiliary Bishop with responsibilities for the welfare of the children in the Catholic community of his region, to take such action as he could to advocate that Father Searson be removed or suspended or, at least, that a thorough investigation be undertaken of the allegations. It was the same responsibility that attached to other Auxiliary Bishops and the Vicar General when they received complaints.

Bishop Pell was the Auxiliary Bishop to the Archbishop. He had the capacity and opportunity to urge the Archbishop to take action against Father Searson in order to protect the children of the parish and the Catholic community of his region. Cardinal Pell's evidence was that he could not recall recommending a particular course of action to the Archbishop. He conceded that, in retrospect, he might have been 'a bit more pushy' with all the parties involved. We do not accept any qualification that this conclusion is only appreciable in retrospect. On the basis of what was known to Bishop Pell in 1989, it ought to have been obvious to him at the time. He should have advised the Archbishop to remove Father Searson and he did not do so.[24]

Much was made in the commission report about whether the Catholic Education Office was providing Pell with sufficient information about Searson's wrongdoings and what possible motivations there may have been for the Catholic Education Office to withhold information. The commission found Pell's theory about why the CEO acted in this way implausible. But nothing turned on that anyway.

Once again I find Pell's statement of 7 May 2020 to be accurate and the commission's findings somewhat equivocal and poorly reasoned.

I suspect that the Holy See would have had a thorough assessment made of the royal commission findings against Pell. I suspect, like me, would have been quite unimpressed by the forensic quality of the commission's work. I suspect that the Pell supporters in Rome

---

[24]   Ibid, pp. 116-7

would have indicated to all and sundry behind closed doors that the commission was out to get Pell. I suspect that Pope Francis with his lifetime of experience in Argentina would have decided it was time to show his support for Pell as one marked out for unfair treatment by people exercising the authority of the state.

Once again, the failings of state officials compound further the hurt to victims of abuse and frustrate further the possibility of the church and its leadership being able to get on with the real work of truth, justice and healing.

Having revisited the commission reports, I think Pope Francis did the right thing.

Let's continue to pray for the victims who presume the royal commissioners were competent and objective and who hope that Pope Francis 'gets it' and is able to effect the ongoing reforms our Church so desperately needs.

14

Where Has Cardinal Pell's Case Brought Us in the Australian Church?

Studies: An Irish Quarterly Review

Spring 2021[25]

Pope John Paul II's biographer George Weigel writing the Introduction to Cardinal Pell's *Prison Journal* describes this writer as one who 'had previously held no brief for Cardinal Pell' and as 'one who was a severe critic'.[26] I plead guilty to both charges. Nevertheless, having attended parts of his two criminal trials and having studied all the publicly available transcript, I am convinced of Pell's innocence of

---

[25]   *Studies*, volume 110, Number 437, pp. 36-51

[26]   George Weigel, Introduction, in George Pell, *Prison Journal*, Volume 1, Ignatius Press, San Francisco, p.8. For example on 3 June 2015 I had published these comments: 'Let me be very upfront. I am no fan of Pell, and he is no fan of mine. It got to the stage a few years ago that he published a gratuitous defamation of me and the Jesuits. He said: "Part of the key to understanding Brennan is that he's really not well-educated in the Catholic tradition" and that with the Jesuits, Jesus "has been almost displaced by (their) enthusiasm for social justice". I asked for an apology. Not only was none forthcoming, he wrote to me saying, "I am afraid that your letter confirms my worst fears about your judgment and about the absence of a proper sense of respect for, and understanding of, things Catholic. This has nothing to do with postgraduate credentials, no reflection on your integrity, but touches on your Catholic sensibilities."' See Frank Brennan, 'It doesn't help to condemn George Pell', *The Australian*, 3 June 2015.

the criminal charges he faced and I am further convinced that the Australian Royal Commission failed to accord him natural justice in their pursuit of a necessary big scalp for media delectation. Pell is a culture warrior inside and outside the Church. In this role, he has triumphed; and in this role, he has suffered. I am a Jesuit who has adopted positions at odds with him inside and outside the Church, and I probably will again. I am happy to respond to the question from the *Studies* editor: 'Where Has Cardinal Pell's Case Brought Us in the Australian Church?' The Australian Church, whether Pell supporters or Pell critics, are trying to move on from the trauma and publicity of trials and media titillation about all but impossible criminal sexual activity in a cathedral sacristy immediately after solemn mass. The trauma and titillation have been fuelled by incompetent policing, improper prosecution, shoddy journalism, judicial failure, and nefarious Vatican financial transactions.

Since the Royal Commission into Institutional Responses to Child Sexual Abuse, there have been some necessary reforms. Laws have been enacted making it easier for complainants to bring civil proceedings claiming damages against the Church for child sexual abuse by clergy and church personnel. The civil law now guarantees that a plaintiff has access to an entity capable of being sued. The usual limitation period of six years after attainment of adulthood has been removed. And deeds of release from liability can be overridden if a court thinks it just and reasonable to do so. These are welcome legal reforms. Victims not wanting to sue can access a government administered national redress scheme similar to those set up by the Church in the last 30 years, but with no church involvement in the administration or determination of claims. The royal commission trumpeted this reform, but victims are finding government bureaucrats no better than church bureaucrats in processing their claims.

Since the royal commission and Pell trials, the Church has lost most of its public standing and credibility when agitating for justice and the common good. Thus, church leaders tend to confine their advocacy to matters relevant only to the Church's own self-interest over against the state. Secularists welcome this development, but it probably means reduced advocacy for the poorest and most marginalised members of society. There are times when a Church voice can help. Or at least it did in the past.

Pell faced criminal trials which were conducted under suppression orders. This meant the public was not able to follow the evidence in the trials day by day. The public was simply presented with a final verdict followed by an internationally live televised public sentencing at which the trial judge had to operate on the basis that the jury had made the right decision. Once the suppression orders were lifted, three books with popular appeal were published, all critical of Pell and the Church.[27] Only now are books more attentive to the evidence and therefore supportive of Pell starting to appear.[28] Pell has published his *Prison Journal* and conducted an international media campaign aimed at restoring his standing, particularly with the more conservative Catholics in the USA and the UK.

Cardinal Pell: some background

Cardinal Pell is the Australian of all time who has been most highly promoted in the Catholic Church. We Australians are noted for our egalitarianism and our irreverence towards those in authority. It's known as the tall poppy syndrome. Any poppy that grows too tall is cut down to the size of others in the field. Pell has long been a divisive figure in the Catholic Church in Australia. In 1987, he became auxiliary bishop of his home diocese Melbourne aged 46 having completed doctoral studies at Oxford in the early 1970s. From 1988 on, the Australian Catholic Bishops Conference was regularly discussing how best to deal with sexual abuse by clergy and religious. After nine years as auxiliary to Archbishop Sir Frank Little with

---

[27] Louise Milligan, *Cardinal: The Rise and Fall of George Pell*, Melbourne University Press, 2017; Lucie Morris-Marr, *Fallen*, Allen & Unwin, 2019; Melissa Davey, *The Case of George Pell*, Scribe, 2020

[28] Keith Windschuttle, *The Persecution of George Pell*, Quadrant Books, 2020; Gerard Henderson's book is forthcoming in April 2021.

whom he had a rather distant relationship, Pell was made archbishop of Melbourne overnight in 1996 when Little was effectively sacked, in part for his failure to deal adequately with issues of child sexual abuse. On the urging of prominent civic leaders including the state governor and premier, Pell acted immediately to set up 'the Melbourne Response' for dealing with allegations of abuse by church personnel. He set up expert panels which paid compensation in the same range as the state provided for victims of crime. Professional counselling was also provided. He acted unilaterally while the other Australian bishops set up a national protocol called 'Towards Healing'. Many in the Church thought this unilateral action was typical of Pell and they were critical of him for not being a team player. But state leaders and the Victoria Police were quite complimentary about the Pell initiative. He had acted resolutely, quickly and professionally. Victims and their supporters were critical. Some who met with Pell thought him to be lacking in empathy.

In 2001 Pope John Paul II took the unprecedented step of transferring the Archbishop of Melbourne, in this case George Pell, to Sydney. Sydney traditionally carried the red hat and Pell was elevated to the college of Cardinals in 2003. From there, Pell was appointed to some of the Vatican dicasteries and travelled regularly to Rome. In 2014, he was appointed to a full-time position in Rome as the Prefect of the Secretariat for the Economy. While his ecclesiastical promotions were boundless, his problems back home compounded.

In 2002, a person had alleged that Pell when a seminarian had sexually abused him as a child at a parish holiday camp. Neither the 'Towards Healing' nor Melbourne Response protocols had been designed to deal with a complaint against an archbishop. A non-Catholic retired judge was appointed by the Church to conduct an investigation. The judge concluded: 'I accept as correct the submission ... that the complainant, when giving evidence of molesting, gave the impression that he was speaking honestly from an actual recollection. However, the respondent, also, gave me the impression that he was speaking the truth. In the end, and notwithstanding that impression of the complainant, bearing in mind the forensic difficulties of the defence occasioned by the very long delay, some valid criticism of the complainant's credibility, the lack of corroborative evidence and the sworn denial of the respondent, I find I am not "satisfied that the complaint has been established", to quote the words of the principal term of reference. I so advise the appointors.'[29] Pell's supporters claimed he was vindicated; his critics said that he was under a cloud. Thereafter, some victims and their supporters had Pell in the gun. When unseemly details of the criminal record of the complainant later came to light, Pell's supporters were adamant that the allegations were fabricated or fantasised.

Pell continued to exercise firm leadership in the Church. He proudly proclaimed his theological conservatism and expressed displeasure at the musings of those he regarded as theological liberals. Inside and outside the Church, he was a lightning rod conductor for controversy.

Ten years after Pell had left Melbourne, the government, police and church actors who had signed off on the Melbourne Response had all moved on. There was a growing public awareness of the problem of child sexual abuse within institutions. In Victoria there were a few priests by then known to be notorious paedophiles who had violated many, many children. Two institutions were at fault, failing to act on information previously available to them – the Victoria Police and the Catholic Church. The Victoria Police decided that attack was the best form of defence. On 29 September 2011, Deputy Police Commissioner Graham Ashton sent a letter to the Church, stating that Police could no longer publicly support a new protocol which had been developed with the Church. The Victorian Parliament announced an inquiry into abuse on 17 April 2012. In its final report published on 13 November 2013, the parliamentary committee unanimously observed: 'It is clear that Victoria Police paid inadequate attention to the fundamental problems of the Melbourne Response arrangements until relatively recently in April 2012 and that, when they did become the subject

---

[29]   A J Southwell QC, *Report of an Inquiry into an Allegation of Sexual Abuse Against Archbishop George Pell*, 2002, p.15.

of public attention, Victoria Police representatives endeavoured quite unfairly to distance the organisation from them.'[30] Victoria Police had been less than candid.[31]

At the parliamentary inquiry, Pell expressed strong, unqualified criticism of the deceased Archbishop Sir Frank Little for his failure to deal with abuse issues between 1987 and 1996. In his written submission, Pell stated: 'As an auxiliary bishop to Archbishop Little I did not have the authority to handle these matters and had only some general impressions about the response that was being made at that time, but this was sufficient to make it clear to me that this was an issue which needed urgent attention and that we needed to do much better in our response.'[32]

The public was left wondering if Pell had information or reasonable suspicions about child sexual abuse by clergy in the Melbourne Archdiocese prior to his archiepiscopal appointment in July 1996, and why he had no authority and was unable to act on any information he had obtained prior to that appointment. He conceded to the Victorian Inquiry, 'At this time, the media was full of accounts detailing sex abuse in the Catholic community.'[33] This left some people wondering, 'If Little didn't act, why didn't Pell?' and 'If Little knew, surely Pell must have too.' As an auxiliary bishop, Pell said he was left in the dark. Prior to 1996, things were a mess. For nine of those years, Pell was an

---

[30]   Victorian Parliament, Family and Community Development Committee, *Betrayal of Trust Inquiry into The Handling of Child Abuse by Religious and Other Non-Government Organisations*, Final Report, 2013, p.25

[31]   When questioned by his favourite radio interviewer Neil Mitchell about this criticism of the Victoria Police by the parliamentary inquiry, Commissioner Ashton claimed on 20 November 2013: 'We certainly though didn't wait for the Parliamentary inquiry before we voiced our concerns. I think it may have said in the report that we only sort of distanced ourselves once this inquiry started. Well, we did raise the flag, and indeed I was on your show talking about this prior to the report being published.' Mitchell intervened saying, 'Yeah, well you said that they had reported nothing, that the... You stand by all that?' Ashton continued, 'Stand by everything in the report. The Parliamentary report didn't criticise any of the evidence in our report, so yeah, we stand by that.'

[32]   Cardinal George Pell, Submission to Victorian Parliament, Family and Community Development Committee, 24 May 2013, p.2. Archbishop Little had died in April 2008.

[33]   Ibid

auxiliary bishop in Melbourne. Only his archbishop was superior to him in the archdiocesan power structure. Pell told the 2013 Victorian parliamentary inquiry, 'When I was Auxiliary Bishop of Melbourne I was not a part of the system or procedures for dealing with paedophilia.'[34] By 1988, he like anyone else attentive to media reports was aware that there was a problem and that there were 'terrible situations, for example, in Canada'[35]. In 1988, Pell's superior, Archbishop Little had set up a confidential subcommittee to deal with abuse complaints. Membership included a couple of clergy, a barrister and a psychiatrist. Pell says he knew nothing of their deliberations. In 1993, a Pastoral Response Office (PRO) was set up in the archdiocese. Pell says, 'Prior to my appointment as Archbishop, I had little if any involvement with the PRO.'[36]

The Royal Commission

The Commonwealth Government then set up a five-year national royal commission to look into these matters. Since the damning findings of that royal commission, the Australian Church has had to accept moral responsibility and legal liability for all child sexual abuse committed by clergy prior to 1996, regardless of what might be the moral or legal position after 1996 when improved measures for supervision and dismissal of errant clergy were put in place. In relation to any abuse occurring before 1996, there is no way that the Church can argue that it had structures in place which gave priority to the well-being of vulnerable children.

The royal commission needed a big scalp, and Pell's was the one they wanted. They set up various lines of inquiry to get him. In his sworn statement to the royal commission in August 2014, Cardinal Pell said, 'During the period in which I was Auxiliary Bishop from 1987 to 1996, I did not myself have any direct responsibility for handling is-

---

[34] Hansard, Family and Community Development Committee, 27 May 2013, p. 7.
[35] Ibid.
[36] George Pell, Witness Statement to Royal Commission into Institutional Responses to Child Sexual Abuse, 7 August 2014, p.5.

sues relating to child sexual abuse. It was not my role to assist Arch-bishop Little in managing these matters.'[37] He told the Commission, 'I wasn't in the direct line of authority before I was Archbishop. I was an Auxiliary Bishop with no responsibility in this area.'[38]

Australian Catholics have had to accept that, at least until 1996 when the new protocols were introduced, they were members of a social institution so hazily structured that not even one as savvy as Cardinal Pell was expected to know or do anything conclusive about alleged child sexual abuse, regardless of how high he had escalated the ec-clesiastical pyramid. He had been a priest and consultor in a country diocese (Ballarat) where abuse was rampant, rector of the Melbourne seminary when abuse in some of the Melbourne parishes was fre-quent, and then auxiliary bishop for nine years when clerical sexual abuse was being constantly discussed in the mainstream media. He conceded that there was 'significant truth' in the suggestion that a 'systemic cover-up allowed paedophile priests to prey on innocent children'.[39]

In future, Church morale will be enhanced if the anti-Pell forces in-side and outside the Church are willing to concede that bishops like Pell got some things right when it came to the protection of children after 1996, and they were ahead of the curve. Ongoing universal con-demnation of initiatives like the Melbourne Response and 'Towards Healing' does little to effect the future protection of children. Twenty five years on, everyone has learnt better processes and the state has imposed more rigorous regulation and supervision.

During the conduct of the National Royal Commission, the Victoria Police commenced an operation on Christmas Eve 2015 seeking ev-idence of any wrongdoing by Pell around his cathedral during the years 1996-2001 when he was Archbishop of Melbourne. This ex-traordinary trawling exercise which included front page newspaper stories at Christmas time failed to produce any real leads for the po-

---

[37] Ibid
[38] Transcript, Royal Commission into Institutional Responses to Child Sexual Abuse, 21 August 2014, p. C4525
[39] Hansard, Family and Community Development Committee, 27 May 2013, pp. 13-14

lice. Five months previously, the ultimate complainant in the only Pell trials had given two statements to police. The police may have put his case on hold, hoping to turn up something more compelling with their broad-ranging inquiries. The complainant ultimately gave evidence that he and his now deceased companion were sexually assaulted by Pell in the priests' sacristy at the cathedral immediately after solemn Sunday mass in St Patrick's Cathedral in late 1996. He detailed a series of sexual assaults which would have lasted at least 5-6 minutes. He also gave evidence that Pell assaulted him in the crowded sacristy corridor after another mass a couple of months later.

Pell was charged by police in June 2017, almost two years after the complainant had made his two statements to police. Pell was committed by a magistrate to stand trial in May 2018. At the first trial in the County Court of Victoria, the jury could not agree and was discharged in September 2018. At the second trial he was convicted on 11 December 2018. All legal proceedings had been subject to suppression orders until his sentencing hearing in February 2019. His appeal to the Victorian Court of Appeal was heard in June 2019 and dismissed on 21 August 2019. His appeal to the High Court of Australia was heard in March 2020. On 7 April 2020, the Tuesday of Holy Week, all seven High Court justices upheld his appeal. Ultimately Pell was acquitted of all charges. The charges should never have come to court.

The High Court of Australia's findings

The High Court of Australia unanimously ruled in relation to all five charges, 'there is a significant possibility that an innocent person has been convicted'[40]. The court ordered that Pell's 'convictions be quashed and judgments of acquittal be entered in their place'[41].

The court accepted that the jury had assessed the complainant's evidence 'as thoroughly credible and reliable'[42]. In the Victorian Court of Appeal, that step was enough for two of the judges erroneously

---

[40] *Pell* v *The Queen* [2020] HCA 12 (7 April 2020), paras 119, 127, available at http://eresources.hcourt.gov.au/showCase/2020/HCA/12.

[41] Ibid, para 129

[42] Ibid, para 39

to uphold the convictions. But the dissenting judge, Mark Weinberg, Australia's most experienced criminal appeal court judge, thought that was only the first step of a court's inquiry, and not the last. All seven High Court judges agreed. The court needed to examine the record of all the evidence in the case 'to see whether, notwithstanding that assessment, the court is satisfied that the jury, acting rationally, ought nonetheless to have entertained a reasonable doubt as to proof of guilt'[43]. The High Court unanimously decided that any jury acting rationally must have had a reasonable doubt.

In addition to the complainant, there were many other witnesses called by the prosecution in Pell's case. They included 23 witnesses who were involved in the conduct of solemn mass at the Cathedral or who were members of the choir in 1996 and/or 1997. Many of these witnesses were also thoroughly credible and quite reliable, though their reliability faltered at times given that they were trying to recall what they would have been doing after mass in St Patrick's Cathedral on a particular Sunday 22 years before. The honesty of these witnesses was not questioned by the prosecution.

The High Court found that many of these witnesses had given consistent evidence that placed Pell on the steps of the Cathedral for at least 10 minutes after mass on 15 and 22 December 1996, the only possible dates when the first four offences could have been committed. The prosecution 'conceded that the offences alleged in the first incident could not have been committed if, following mass, (Pell) had stood on the Cathedral steps greeting congregants for ten minutes.'[44]

The court also found that there was unquestioned evidence by honest witnesses that placed Pell in company with his Master of Ceremonies when he returned to the priests' sacristy to disrobe. Furthermore, there was abundant evidence of 'continuous traffic into and out of the priests' sacristy for ten to 15 minutes' after the altar servers returned to the sacristy at the end of the procession at the conclusion of mass.[45]

---

[43] Ibid
[44] Ibid, para 54
[45] Ibid, para 118.

There was no 5-6 minute hiatus for the offences to occur straight after mass – with Pell, the complainant and his companion in the sacristy alone, together and uninterrupted.

When interviewed in Rome back in October 2016 by Victorian police officers who were being supervised by their Deputy Commissioner Shane Patton, Pell told the police that the sacristy was 'a hive of activity' after mass with altar servers, sacristan, assistant sacristan, money collectors and any concelebrating priests coming and going. He said he would have been accompanied at all relevant times by his MC Monsignor Charles Portelli. He also told the police that the usual course after a solemn mass was for everyone to process down the main aisle of the cathedral, then processing externally for some minutes around the cathedral, back into the sacristy area. This was news to the police investigators. The complainant had never mentioned an external procession. This made the whole police case suspect as there was a need for the complainant to have time to leave the external procession making his way to the sacristy before the altar servers and concelebrants arrived. But then, there was no way that Pell could also have got there before the others in the procession.

The police returned to Australia and interviewed Portelli and the sacristan Max Potter who basically confirmed all that Pell had said about the 'hive of activity' and the external procession. Despite (or perhaps, because of) the now obvious incoherence of the complainant's account, the police did not bother to interview one single altar server. They made no inquiries about money collectors or concelebrating priests. They proceeded to charge Pell – with great media fanfare. They went ahead building a case on the basis that the priests' sacristy might have been left vacant and open on this one particular day – contrary to all church routine and ritual. Yet the High Court rightly observed that 'adherence to ritual and compliance with established liturgical practice is a defining feature of religious observance.'[46]

The farce of the case was the belated and contorted attempt by the Director of Public Prosecutions (DPP) to create the space for the nec-

---

[46]   Ibid, para 93.

essary 5-6 minute hiatus. At trial, the prosecutor had suggested, contrary to the evidence, that the altar servers might have adjourned to another room, for no reason, for 5-6 minutes before being called back to the priests' sacristy to resume their duties at the end of mass. He had to withdraw that suggestion before the jury. He even suggested that the fully vested MC might have popped outside for a cigarette leaving Pell to his own devices. There was no evidence of this. The MC had denied it. The prosecutor had to withdraw the suggestion. In the High Court, the DPP submitted once again that the servers might have adjourned to another room or to the sanctuary to assist the sacristan. The High Court dealt with this suggestion kindly but firmly: 'The submission comes close to repeating the submission which the prosecutor withdrew at the trial. There was no evidence that the altar servers went to their room to disrobe prior to returning to the sanctuary in order to assist in clearing away the sacred vessels and other objects.'[47]

The complainant had alleged a second incident when Pell assaulted him in the sacristy corridor immediately after mass with many altar servers and choristers in the vicinity, both adults and children. The police knew the identity of Brendan Egan the priest who celebrated that mass and who was standing immediately in front of Pell who was presiding. To this day, the police have never spoken to Egan who later left the priesthood and who has been living and working in Melbourne as the Social Wellbeing Program Manager at a local council. The police did not interview a single person other than the complainant about this second alleged incident. Presumably they knew they would not find any credible evidence warranting a conviction on this charge.

The High Court adopted the same approach as Justice Weinberg, the dissenting judge in the Victorian Court of Appeal, who 'considered that, had the second incident occurred in the way [the complainant] described it, it was highly unlikely that none of the many persons present would have seen what was happening or reported it in some way.'[48] The seven High Court justices observed: 'The assumption that

---

[47] Ibid, para 117.
[48] Ibid, para 123

a group of choristers, including adults, might have been so preoccupied with making their way to the robing room as to fail to notice the extraordinary sight of the Archbishop of Melbourne dressed "in his full regalia" advancing through the procession and pinning a 13 year old boy to the wall, is a large one. The failure to make any formal report of such an incident, had it occurred, may be another matter.'[49]

This second incident should have sounded to the police like the 13th strike of a clock, alerting them that the complainant's recollection of events was fundamentally wrong, regardless of his apparent honesty and credibility. The police simply wanted the media fanfare of pressing the charges regardless of the incoherence of the evidence and regardless of the advice from the office of prosecutions. Announcing the charges, Deputy Commissioner Patton (since promoted to Chief Commissioner replacing Mr Ashton) told the media: 'Advice was received and sought from the Office of Public Prosecutions, however ultimately the choice to charge Cardinal Pell was one that was made by Victoria Police.'[50]

In the end, there was just not the evidence to support the complainant's account of either incident. There never was. Those Australians who neither canonise nor despise George Pell can be grateful that the High Court has finally delivered justice according to law in this absurd, protracted Victorian saga. Not even the three journalists who have published anti-Pell books on the trial have been able to formulate a theory, let alone evidence, as to how and when there could have been 5-6 minutes after mass when the complainant and his companion could have been alone with Pell in the sacristy.

---

49   Ibid, para 124. When interviewed about this second incident by Paul Kelly after the High Court decision, I said, 'The fragility of the Victorian criminal justice system is exposed when you look at the total absence of any investigation of the second incident and the reasoning of Ferguson and Maxwell satisfying themselves that the incident must have occurred. I don't think Aborigines were treated as prejudicially by even the worst of the 19th-century judges.' See Paul Kelly, 'Travesty of Justice', *Weekend Australian*, 11-12 April 2020.

50   Shane Patton, Victoria Police statement concerning charges against Cardinal George Pell, 29 June 2017

After the case

Speaking of the complainant in these proceedings, Pell told the BBC on 20 December 2020: 'His memory is certainly fallible. He changed his story 24 times. But he did construct for himself a perfect alibi. So by his own accounts, he could not have been in the sacristy being attacked while he was still in procession. Not even a credible witness can be in two places at once.'[51] The complainant is understood to have been sexually abused as a child first by a family friend when baby sitting and then by a parish priest when he was an altar server. There is no reason to doubt that he has been a victim of sexual abuse. There is every reason to doubt that he was abused by Pell on two occasions immediately after mass in the cathedral. The police and his supporters should have spared the complainant the trauma of these proceedings. Thankfully Pell has said, 'I hold no ill will toward my accuser, I do not want my acquittal to add to the hurt and bitterness so many feel; there is certainly hurt and bitterness enough. The only basis for long term healing is truth and the only basis for justice is truth, because justice means truth for all.'[52] The complainant issued a statement through his lawyers saying, 'My journey has been long and I am relieved that it is over. I have my ups and downs. The darkness is never far away. Despite the stress of the legal process and public controversy I have tried hard to keep myself together. I am OK. I hope that everyone who has followed this case is OK.'[53]

The Victoria Police have a lot to answer for. They were not helped by the DPP nor by the two Victorian appeal court judges who made basic, lamentable errors in their judgment. Recently another royal commission has concluded, finding that over 100 Victoria Police were aware that a defence barrister was being used as a human source in police investigations into that barrister's clients. The High Court of Australia said:

> Victoria Police were guilty of reprehensible conduct in knowingly

---

[51] BBC4, *Sunday*, 20 December 2020 available at https://www.bbc.co.uk/programmes/m000qhft
[52] Statement by Cardinal Pell, 7 April 2020
[53] Statement by Mr J, issued by his lawyer Ms V Waller, 7 April 2020

encouraging [the defence barrister] to do as she did and were involved in sanctioning atrocious breaches of the sworn duty of every police officer to discharge all duties imposed on them faithfully and according to law without favour or affection, malice or ill-will. As a result, the prosecution of each Convicted Person was corrupted in a manner which debased fundamental premises of the criminal justice system.[54]

When asked on radio by his favourite talk show host about the High Court decision, Commissioner Ashton responded:[55]

MR MITCHELL: She [the defence barrister] went through 'til 2010 which was after the gangland wars.

MR ASHTON: ... there was significant underworld activity right through that period as well.

MR MITCHELL: It's the old argument that the end justifies the means.

MR ASHTON: The question is what was the means and what was wrong with the means.

MR MITCHELL: The High Court had a view that it was atrocious behaviour by Vic Pol.

MR ASHTON: And the courts have a view about this all the way through ... it doesn't mean that we don't take a slightly different view of that.

MR MITCHELL: You take a slightly different view to the High Court of Australia?

MR ASHTON: Yeah.

The brazenness of this police response is highlighted by the commission's conclusion 'that the convictions or findings of guilt of 1,011 people may have been affected by Victoria Police's use of

---

54 *AB (a pseudonym) v CD (a pseudonym); EF (a pseudonym) v CD (a pseudonym)* (2018) 362 *Australian Law Reports* 1, 4 [10] (Kiefel CJ, Bell, Gageler, Keane, Nettle, Gordon and Edelman JJ).

55 Neil Mitchell, 3AW, Transcript of Chief Commissioner Graham Ashton's 3AW interview, 28 March 2019, 2–3.

[the defence barrister] as a human source'.[56] The Victorian courts will spend the next decade determining whether convicted criminals should be released from jail because their trials were irredeemably tainted by corrupt police practices. For this reason, some long term prisoners have already walked free.

Mr Ashton prior to becoming police commissioner had headed the force's Office of Police Integrity (OPI). The royal commission found:

> Mr Ashton may not have known the full extent of [the defence barrister's] duplicitous role, but ...he knew she was a criminal defence barrister who had operated for an extended period as a Victoria Police human source under the supervision of the SDU (Source Development Unit). He should have known that this inherently problematic situation warranted urgent legal advice as to its propriety and that it may very well raise issues requiring the OPI's investigation and oversight. Mr Ashton's omission to investigate the propriety of [the barrister's] use as a human source was a lost opportunity for the OPI to perform its independent oversight function.[57]

When Cardinal Pell was acquitted of all charges and when all other charges were dropped by the DPP, Pell's critics turned to the adverse findings against him in the long running Royal Commission into Institutional Responses to Child Sexual Abuse. The Commission made a number of adverse findings about whether Pell knew or should have known about instances of child sexual abuse first when he was a diocesan consultor as a priest in Ballarat and then as an auxiliary bishop in Melbourne. There was no conclusive evidence to warrant such findings. The commissioners made a number of observations that Pell's denials were 'implausible'. Unfortunately for the commission, his denials were not only consistent with the evidence of other witnesses but also with the findings made by the commission in relation to those other witnesses. Cardinal Pell issued this spare and

---

[56] Margaret McMurdo, Royal Commission into the Management of Police Informants, *Final Report*, November 2020, p. 17

[57] Ibid, p. 136

accurate statement on 7 May 2020 when the findings were published:

> Cardinal Pell said he was surprised by some of the views of the Royal Commission about his actions. These views are not supported by evidence.
>
> He is especially surprised by the statements in the report about the earlier transfers of Gerald Ridsdale discussed by the Ballarat Diocesan Consultors in 1977 and 82.
>
> The Consultors who gave evidence on the meetings in 1977 and 1982 either said they did not learn of Ridsdale's offending against children until much later or they had no recollection of what was discussed. None said they were made aware of Ridsdale's offending at these meetings.
>
> The then Fr Pell left the Diocese of Ballarat and therefore his position as a consultor at the end of 1984.
>
> As an Auxiliary Bishop in Melbourne 1987-96, Bishop Pell met with a delegation from Doveton Parish in 1989 which did not mention sexual assaults and did not ask for Searson's removal.
>
> Appointed Archbishop of Melbourne on 16 August 1996, Archbishop Pell placed Fr Searson on administrative leave in March 1997 and removed him from the parish on 15 May 1997.[58]

In conclusion

The Australian Church continues to deal with the legacy of George Pell who like many other Australians prior to 1996 had little sensitivity to the pervasive reality of child sexual abuse in institutions and did little to ensure that such abuse could not occur within institutions. No doubt the legacy would be easier to bear if Pell had worked closely with all his fellow bishops when designing the first protocols. The public ignominy would have been less if he had returned to Australia

---

[58] George Pell, Media Release, 7 May 2020, available at https://tinyurl.com/yuye7dbu

to front the royal commission, rather than remaining in Rome for his third appearance by video link at night time. People thought he had something to hide. He would have had a better chance of the jury acquitting him in the first instance if he had gone into the witness box subjecting himself to strenuous cross-examination as had the complainant. Australians now have a low tolerance of bishops employing tough defence counsel to cross-examine complainants while the bishops sit mute.

Pell paid for these mistakes with 404 days of wrongful imprisonment, much of it in solitary confinement. The time has come to attest that Pell worked tirelessly and to the best of his ability from 1996 to put right the dreadful consequences of institutional child sexual abuse. It's time to call out Mr Ashton who when asked by Mr Mitchell what he thought of claims Victoria Police were out to 'get' Pell replied, 'What a joke. We don't run vendettas against people, that's not what we're about, that's not why we take an oath.'[59] The police vendetta against Pell ran for years. Pell faced charges which were false, a prosecution which was malicious, a Victorian appeal court which failed to administer justice according to law in the face of a baying crowd, a media campaign which was relentlessly prejudiced, and royal commission findings which demonstrably failed to accord natural justice.

Attitudes have changed about all manner of things in Australia since 1996. There have been six prime ministers since Pell was first made an archbishop. In our Westminster style parliaments, elected leaders from both sides of politics turn over with sufficient rapidity that they are not held personally responsible for institutional failures of previous generations. A bishop embodies functions of both politician and civil servant. Bishops like Pell who preside over dioceses for decades come to embody the institution, including its failures. Pell has been emblematic of the Australian Catholic Church for decades.

Catholics continue to be identified as pro-Pell or anti-Pell. I am convinced of his innocence, though I still don't subscribe to his culture

---

[59] Neil Mitchell, 3AW, Chief Commissioner Graham Ashton's 3AW interview 9 April 2020, at https://tinyurl.com/wc5at2u9

wars. I've come to enjoy his company and admire his resolute courage. We will continue to disagree over matters like the primacy of the formed and informed conscience, the theological possibility of papal approval of women's ordination, and the jurisprudential justification for civil laws recognising the unions of same sex couples and describing them as marriage. I do hope for the good of the Australian Church that the intrigue about Vatican financial scandals will abate and Pell's influence over episcopal appointments will wane. On 8 June 2021, Pell turns 80. He will no longer be eligible to vote at conclave. He will stand for the rest of his days as a distinctive Australian crossbreed of sacrificial lamb and scapegoat wearing a tall poppy fleece.

In October 2021, the Australian Catholic Church responding to Pope Francis' call for a more synodal Church will convene the first session of its Plenary Council marking the beginning of the post-Pell era. Announcing the appointment of the Plenary Council executive, Archbishop Mark Coleridge, President of the Australian Catholic Bishops Conference, said 'This is no time for the Church to be putting up signs that say "business as usual". If we needed any proof, then the Royal Commission has shown that. We need to face the facts, and in the light of the facts, which aren't always friendly, we have to make big decisions about the future. The Plenary Council will place the Church on a sound footing to respond to what is not merely an era of change but a change of era.'[60] No doubt, George Cardinal Pell, though absent, will be praying that the Spirit remains alive and active during this change of era in *Terra Australis*, the Great South Land of the Holy Spirit.

---

[60] Archbishop Mark Coleridge, Media Release, Appointment of Plenary Council Executive Committee, 28 June 2017

Observations after the Publication of the Book's First Edition

15

'I'm a critic but George Pell really was treated unjustly'

The Australian

7 April 2021

Pope John Paul II's biographer George Weigel, writing the introduction to Cardinal George Pell's Prison Journal, describes me as one who 'had previously held no brief for Cardinal Pell (and) a severe critic'. I plead guilty.

Nevertheless, having attended parts of his two criminal trials and having studied all the publicly available transcript, I am convinced of Pell's innocence of the criminal charges he faced. I am convinced the Royal Commission into Institutional Responses to Child Sexual Abuse failed to accord him natural justice in its pursuit of a necessary big scalp for media delectation.

Australia's Catholic Church continues to deal with the legacy of Pell, who like many other Australians before 1996 – when he set up the Melbourne Response protocol to deal with abuse allegations – had little sensitivity to the pervasive reality of child sexual abuse in institutions and did little to ensure abuse could not occur within such settings.

No doubt the legacy would be easier to bear if Pell had worked closely with all his fellow bishops when designing the first protocols. The public ignominy would have been less if he had returned to Australia to front the royal commission rather than remaining in Rome for his third appearance by video link at night-time. People thought he had something to hide.

He would have had a better chance of the jury acquitting him in the first instance if he had gone into the witness box, subjecting himself to strenuous cross-examination, as had the complainant. Australians now have a low tolerance of bishops employing tough defence counsel to cross-examine complainants while the bishops sit mute.

Pell paid for these mistakes with 404 days of wrongful imprisonment, much of it in solitary confinement. The time has come to attest that Pell worked tirelessly and to the best of his ability from 1996 to put right the dreadful consequences of institutional child sexual abuse. Pell faced charges that should never have been brought, a prosecution that was malicious, a Victorian appeal court that got it very wrong, and a media campaign that was relentlessly prejudiced.

Attitudes have changed about all manner of things since 1996. There have been six prime ministers since Pell was first made an archbishop. In our Westminster-style parliaments, elected leaders from both sides of politics turn over with sufficient rapidity that they are not held personally responsible for institutional failures of previous generations.

A bishop embodies functions of both politician and civil servant. Bishops such as Pell who preside over dioceses for decades come to embody the institution, including its failures. Pell has been emblematic of the Australian Catholic Church for decades.

Catholics continue to be identified as pro-Pell or anti-Pell. Though convinced of his innocence, I still don't subscribe to his culture wars. I've come to enjoy his company and admire his resolute courage. We will continue to disagree over matters such as the theological possibility of papal approval of women's ordination and the jurisprudential justification for civil laws recognising the unions of same-sex couples and describing them as marriage.

I do hope for the good of the Australian church that the intrigue about Vatican financial scandals will abate, and Pell's influence over episcopal appointments will wane. On June 8, Pell turns 80. He will no longer be eligible to vote at conclave. He will stand for the rest of his days as a distinctive Australian crossbreed of sacrificial lamb and scapegoat wearing a tall poppy fleece.

16

Interview on the launching of
Observations on the Pell Proceedings

Sky News

7 April 2021[61]

Kieran Gilbert: Today marks one year since the High Court quashed the child sex abuse convictions of Cardinal George Pell. Cardinal Pell was freed immediately in a single judgement given which held there was a significant possibility that an innocent person has been convicted. Let's bring in Father Frank Brennan who's written lengthy analysis on this, including a book to mark the one year since those convictions were thrown out by the High Court. Frank Brennan, thanks so much for your time. First of all you, write in *The Australian* today[62] and you make the point in your book that you previously weren't a big fan of Cardinal Pell but you did not believe, and having attended the court hearings, that he was guilty of the charges laid against him.

FB: That's correct Kieran, in that Cardinal Pell and I have had all sorts of theological differences in the past and anyone who knows him knows that he can be fairly robust in debate, and yes he had expressed some adverse views of me, and I suppose I had expressed some adverse views of him. But then what we as a nation were confronted

---

[61] See https://www.skynews.com.au/details/_6247391513001

[62] Frank Brennan, 'I'm a critic but George Pell really was treated unjustly', *The Australian*, 7 April 2021, available at https://tinyurl.com/3s48xkuf

with was that he was going to be tried under suppression orders where the public wouldn't have access to the evidence as it unfolded in his cases, and so it was quite clear that I think particularly for Catholics in Australia to have some sense of what was going on, and so I was asked by our bishops whether I could be available to attend some of the proceedings. Cardinal Pell agreed to give me access to the publicly available transcript and out of that I was then able to make some assessment of these things both as a lawyer and as a priest.

KG: And you're also saying that there need to be lessons learned because of the failures of the Victoria police, prosecution authorities, and the two most senior Victorian judges in these proceedings; that there needs to be a better approach that we need to do better.

FB: Yes, well that's why I remain exercised about this Kieran. There are two people who suffered grave injustice as a result of these processes. One was Cardinal Pell who was wrongly imprisoned for 404 days. The other was the complainant who was dealt with by the police and the prosecution authorities in a way where the policing was not adequate, and the prosecution was anything but adequate. And so, what you had was him being put through the trauma of over a year of these proceedings.

See what you've got to remember, if you go back: your listeners, many of whom will remember, that the first report that was given about these alleged incidents was a second-hand report from a journalist Louise Milligan which suggested that somehow these events took place in the back of a cathedral when nobody was around. But it turned out nothing could be further from the truth.[63] What was being alleged was

---

[63]   In 2017, prior to the Pell trials, Louise Milligan published the 1st edition of her book *The Cardinal* (Melbourne University Press, 2017). The complainant resolutely refused to disclose any details of his complaint to Milligan. Milligan proceeded to publish the following hearsay account at p.352:

"The Kid gently told her what he says happened with the Archbishop. 'He told me that himself and [my son] used to play in the back of the Church in the closed-off rooms,' she says.
'In the cathedral?' I ask her.
'In the cathedral, yep. And um, they got sprung by Archbishop Pell and he locked the door and he made them perform oral sex.' The Kid still

that these events took place at the busiest time possible in a cathedral where there would be lots of people around doing just their routine tasks. That required proper policing to see whether or not any charges should be brought.

The other thing to remember Kieran is that the complainant in this case, he went to the police in June 2015. Now the police obviously thought that there was something that didn't quite add up with the case. They were looking for more similar facts sort of evidence. So, they advertised. It was the front page of *The Age* on Christmas Eve. They tried for about a year to see if there were any other complaints. There weren't. There were other complaints about Cardinal Pell in Ballarat, but they went nowhere so in the end this was the only thing left standing.

They went to Rome. They interviewed Cardinal Pell at length and he pointed out to them: he said, 'Look you've got to go back to Melbourne, and you've got to ask the people who would have been there in that sacristy at the time: altar servers, concelebrating priests, money collectors, people like that'. And the police didn't interview any of those people. And the Director of Public Prosecutions didn't ask that that be done. And the Director of Public Prosecutions herself all the way to the High Court of Australia invented evidence in order to try and make up the shortcomings of the case. Now that sort of policing, that sort of prosecution works grave injustice not only on Cardinal Pell, but also on that complainant, and also *bona fide* victims who want to be able to go to the police and be sure that their cases will be properly dealt with. They want to be able to go to the prosecution authorities and make sure they're properly dealt with.

And then on top of that you had the horrendous decision of the two most senior judges in Victoria who were roundly condemned by the High Court for a mode of argument which was just completely

---

remembered the incident so clearly. Being picked up afterwards by his parents. Staring out the car window on the way home."

Key particulars of this hearsay account turned out to be greatly at variance from the evidence presented at the trials.

injudicious.

KG: We've only got a minute left and my apologies as it's a busy news day but in terms of Cardinal Pell's own misjudgements. He should have gone into the witness box and subjected himself to cross examination in your view. There were other misjudgements still. He's had 404 days of wrongful imprisonment you argue.

FB: Well yes, he has. I think he should have gone in the witness box. Obviously, he and his lawyers thought differently, and I mean I wasn't his lawyer. I wasn't on his team. They make their decisions.[64] But I did have a sense that in Australia we had got to the stage, Kieran, the idea that you could have a Cardinal who would have the resources to bring in a heavy hitting lawyer to cross examine a complainant and then not give evidence himself subjecting himself to cross examination. I thought with a jury nowadays that they would be saying why doesn't he just eyeball us and tell us this couldn't possibly be true.

KG: Father Frank Brennan as always, I thank you for your time and your insights into something which has captivated the attention of many around the country. Thank you for that.

FB: Thank you and here's hoping there can be a better way forward for complainants, victims, and anyone who's accused, including those who are wrongly accused in the future.

KG: Father Frank, thanks.

---

[64] In his *Prison Journal*, Cardinal Pell wrote on 19 March 2019: 'Frank Brennan was always keen for me to be in the box, especially after the hung jury decision. Eventually I decided I should give evidence, despite the entire legal team and my own advisers being opposed. Terry Tobin came around to my point of view.

'I only decided not to take the stand after the prosecutor had dealt with Charlie Portelli and especially Max Potter. I was so cross with the treatment they both received, I was frightened that my hostility might turn a majority for acquittal into a split decision. The basis of my reasoning was quite wrong.' George Pell, *Prison Journal*, Volume 1, Ignatius Press, 2020, p. 64.

17

Lessons for Church and State from the Pell Saga

Thomas More Forum, Canberra

25 June 2021[65]

1.   The Example of Thomas More

Mr Bill Mason, Father Emil Milat, ladies and gentlemen: thank you very much for the invitation to return and to address another Thomas More forum. I've entitled tonight's address *Lessons for Church and State from the Pell Saga*. First, the example of Thomas More. When Pope John Paul declared Thomas More a patron of statesmen and politicians he said:

> Whenever men or women heed the call of truth, their conscience then guides their actions reliably towards good. Precisely because of the witness which he bore, even at the price of his life, to the primacy of truth over power, Saint Thomas More is venerated as an imperishable example of moral integrity.' Thomas More 'distinguished himself by his constant fidelity to legitimate authority and institutions precisely in his intention to serve not power but the supreme ideal of justice.' Thomas More 'placed his own public activity at the service of the person, especially if that person was weak or poor;[and] he dealt with social controversies with a superb

---

[65]   The presentation can be viewed at https://www.youtube.com/watch?v=8fJXBuSerZs

sense of fairness'. [66]

Tonight I want to draw lessons from the Pell saga, heeding the call to truth, asserting the primacy of truth over power, working to enhance the place of legitimate authority and institutions which are to be administered not for the sake of power, but to seek the supreme ideal of justice, always having an eye for the one who is weak or poor, and attempting to deal with the most intense of social controversies with a sense of fairness.

2.   The Example of Cardinal Marx and Pope Francis

Second, the example of Cardinal Marx and Pope Francis. As you know, we as a church have been confronting enormous things in relation to child sexual abuse in the church as an institution. Cardinal Marx wrote to Pope Francis on 21 May 2021:

> [It] is important to me to share the responsibility for the catastrophe of the sexual abuse by Church officials over the past decades. The investigations and reports of the last ten years have consistently shown that there have been many personal failures and administrative mistakes but also institutional or 'systemic' failure. The recent debates have shown that some members of the Church refuse to believe that there is a shared responsibility in this respect and that the Church as an institution is hence also to be blamed for what has happened and therefore disapprove of discussing reforms and renewal in the context of the sexual abuse crisis.

> 'I firmly have a different opinion. Both aspects have to be considered: mistakes for which you are personally responsible and the institutional failure which requires changes and a reform of the Church. A turning point out of this crisis is, in my opinion, only possible if we take a "synodal path", a path which actually enables

---

[66]   Pope John Paul II, *Motu Proprio Proclaiming Saint Thomas More Patron of Statesmen and Politicians,* 31 October 2000, available at https://www.vatican.va/content/john-paul-ii/en/motu_proprio/documents/hf_jp-ii_motu-proprio_20001031_thomas-more.pdf

a "discernment of spirits".'

Pope Francis responded on 10 June 2021:

> The whole Church is in crisis because of the abuse issue; Further-
> more, the Church today cannot take a step forward without assum-
> ing this crisis. The ostrich policy does not lead to anything, and the
> crisis has to be assumed from our Easter faith. ... Assuming the
> crisis, personally and communally, is the only fruitful path because
> a crisis does not come out alone but in the community and we must
> also bear in mind that a crisis comes out better or worse, but never
> the same.

3.   The Pell Saga

So I come to consider the case of Cardinal George Pell. This case
impacted most on two individuals - one who is simply known by
the initial 'J', the complainant, and the other, George Pell.   None
of us knows the identity of the complainant in the Pell proceedings;
nor should we. When the High Court acquitted Cardinal Pell of all
charges, the complainant J issued a statement through his lawyer saying, 'My journey has been long, and I am relieved that it is over. I
have my ups and downs. The darkness is never far away. Despite the
stress of the legal process and public controversy I have tried hard
to keep myself together. I am OK. I hope that everyone who has
followed this case is OK.' Earlier, his lawyer Vivian Waller told the
ABC journalist Louise Milligan that J has 'experienced depression,
loneliness struggle with various issues over time' and that 'the criminal process has been quite stressful for him'.[67] Undoubtedly he has
suffered additional trauma through the processes of the law, including
the appeals all the way to the High Court. Much of it was avoidable. These processes have also re-traumatised many other people
who have experienced institutional child sexual abuse and who have
placed hope in our legal system. Their situation would have been

---

[67]   ABC *4 Corners* 'The Conviction of Cardinal Pell', 4 March 1989 available at https://
www.abc.net.au/4corners/guilty:-the-conviction-of-cardinal-pell/10869116

assisted if the police in this case had undertaken competent policing.

Cardinal Pell walked free after 404 days in prison, most often in solitary confinement. When the High Court acquitted him of all charges, he said: 'I hold no ill will towards my accuser. I do not want my acquittal to add to the hurt and bitterness so many feel. There is certainly hurt and bitterness enough. The only basis for long term healing is truth; and the only basis for justice is truth because justice means truth for all.' So I think it behoves us to hold both J and Pell clearly in our sights tonight.

So how did I become involved? Back in 2012 I was giving an address at Parliament House in Sydney. It was the annual *Law and Justice Oration*. I said clearly that the church itself cannot be left alone to get its house in order. I thought the Catholic Church needed the assistance of the state to deal with the issues of child sexual abuse and the failures that had followed institutionally. As all of you would know, Cardinal Pell and I had had our differences and that's to put it mildly. There had been a case running about the late Archbishop Wilson and I thought he was acting with poor advice. When it was clear that any proceedings against Pell were going to be run with suppression orders in place, I was very worried. I had grounds, as I will say later, to be very concerned about the approach of the Victoria Police towards the Catholic Church, but particularly towards George Pell. That being the case, I wrote to Cardinal Pell and I suggested that if he were to be facing trial under suppression orders where the public would not know day-to-day what was occurring, it was essential that there be someone who'd be in a position to inform the public, particularly Catholics of goodwill. Basically I didn't think it should be left just to the ABC and to a few other media outlets. I suggested that he commission the services of a retired County Court judge. In his inimitable style, he came back to me and said, 'I've spoken to my people, and we think it would be better to have you; you'll go over better with the *literati* and the *glitterati*'. So it was arranged that I would play a role, not at the request of Pell but at the request of the President and Vice President of the Australian Catholic Bishops Conference who formally approached the Jesuit Provincial asking for my services to be available to attend what I could of the trials. Pell was to give me access, as he did, to the transcripts.

So I had access to all transcripts except of course the transcript of the complainant giving his evidence. But you will appreciate that most, if not all, of the key evidence of the complainant was either put by the prosecution or the defence to other witnesses, or in their final addresses, or in the judgments of the appeal court judges. It was also decided that I would check in regularly with a very esteemed senior QC of the Melbourne Bar. Day to day as the trial progressed, I would check things out with that QC. I had good relationships with quite a number of professional journalists who were covering the proceedings, and was able to answer some of their queries about the strange nature of a solemn 11:00 AM mass. But I do have to say and disclose that I had nothing to do with the three major book writers simply because none of them ever approached me. In fact, you might be aware that one of them even wrote that I was in the courtroom when the verdict was delivered. I was 1000 kilometres away in Bathurst.

Having attended the proceedings, I think it would be good for everyone, including J and Pell and everyone else who's watched these proceedings, now to declare that truth is the only way to go. It's time to declare that Pell is innocent of the preposterous charges he faced in the County Court of Victoria, and to declare that a lot of grief for everyone including J could have been avoided if there had been competent policing and if there had been competent work by the DPP and if the Victorian Court of Appeal had given a judgment in line with the dissenting judgment of Mark Weinberg, the leading criminal appeal judge in the country or with all seven judges of the highest court in the land.

I published the book *Observations on the Pell Proceedings* so you can make your own assessment of the evidence. The book is dedicated to 'those who seek truth, justice and healing and to those who have been denied them'. Having followed the Pell proceedings closely, I'm convinced that the case did nothing to help *bona fide* complainants; it

135

did nothing to help victims and their supporters. I write in the introduction that 'the failures of the Victorian police, prosecution authorities, and the two most senior Victorian judges in these proceedings did nothing to help the efforts being made to address the trauma of institutional child sexual abuse. As a society we need to do better and the legal system needs to play its part.'

So what was the background? Basically Victoria police charged Pell with 26 offences at the outset. Six of those charges were withdrawn before the committal proceedings. At the committal, the committing magistrate discharged Pell on a further 10 charges. She committed him on 10 remaining charges. Those 10 remaining charges included seven charges in what was alleged to have occurred in Saint Patrick's cathedral and three charges of what was alleged to have occurred in the Ballarat pool. The first moment I smelled a real rat in these proceedings was with the DPP intending to proceed with the Ballarat pool case first when every prosecutorial principle pointed to dealing first with the St Patrick's cathedral charges. They were the far more serious charges involving some very aged witnesses who with the elapsing of time might not have been available and that would have disadvantaged the defendant. It took the defence to put a formal submission that the DPP do its job and apply the honourable principles of prosecution and so then the cathedral case was heard first. Ultimately the Ballarat cases fell over completely because as the County Court judge ruled:

> There is a limit to what the law allows. ... It is one thing to strengthen
> or reinforce individual complaints through the lens of the collective
> weight of the complaints, it is quite another to seek to cure funda-
> mental defects and weaknesses or to change or obscure a complaint's
> essential character. The tendency and coincidence applications seek
> to do the latter here. There is a limit to what can be saved.[68]

So those charges fell over and Pell was never brought to trial on the swimming pool matters. On the Saint Patrick's case, there were five remaining charges - four of which related to an event that was said to

---

[68]   *DPP v Pell (Evidential Ruling No 1)* [2019] VCC 149 para 153

have occurred in the priests' sacristy after solemn 11:00 AM mass, either on 15 December 1996 or 22 December 1996.

Now when we come to consider the truth of the innocence of George Pell, bear this in mind. He was interviewed in Rome on 19 October 2016. Let me quote to you what he said to the police. Now bear in mind, Mr Ashton, the Victorian police commissioner sent none other than his trusted deputy Shane Patton who is now the Commissioner of Police of Victoria. Ashton sent him to Rome to oversee the investigation, and in the record of interview in Rome, this is what Pell said:

> The most rudimentary interview of staff and those who were choir boys at the cathedral in that year and later would confirm that the allegations are fundamentally improbable and most certainly false and I invite my interviewers to tell me who they've spoken to and I'm happy to provide them in due course the persons who can speak authoritatively about my functions, presence and conduct at the cathedral generally and more particularly at times when abuse is alleged to have occurred. I would earnestly hope that this is done before any decision is made whether to lay charges because immeasurable damage will be done to me and to the church by the mere laying of charges which on proper examination will later be found to be untrue. Thank you.[69]

Let's look at a number of vital pieces of evidence from the Pell record of interview. I'm going to focus tonight on the record of interview of Pell in October 2016 because basically it mirrors almost to a sentence the judgment of the seven judges of the High Court of Australia years later in April 2020.

On your tables, you have the list of the raffle prizes, this being a good Catholic event. On the other side of the raffle prizes, you will find a map. The map highlights why I think this case has always been very simple and quite preposterous. If you look at that map, it will make sense to those of you who are familiar with a solemn mass in a cathedral. I can assure you that many of the lawyers in the court were not

---

[69] George Pell, Record of Interview, Rome, 19 October 2016, pp. 9-10.

familiar and I can assure you that many of the media were completely and utterly unfamiliar: 'We don't do Catholic stuff'. If they were having to cover a case which related to a military parade, they'd have learned the ropes saying, 'We've got to get on top of this. This is a military parade.' 'But this is church stuff; now we don't do church stuff.'

So what would happen usually after an 11 AM mass? At the end of mass, the archbishop would leave the sanctuary. There would be as a procession. At the head of the procession would be a number of altar servers, would there not? A cross bearer, 2 candle bearers and probably a couple of others; and then after them would come 50 to 60 choristers; and after them would come any concelebrating priests and the master of ceremonies; and ultimately after them would come the Archbishop with a mitre (the funny hat) and the crozier (a very sacred and very expensive piece of equipment which you just don't leave lying around). He would be accompanied by two additional servers – the mitre bearer and the crozier bearer.

They would all process down the main aisle of the western nave to the steps. They'd make an external procession via the south side of the cathedral and come in what was called the toilet corridor. The concelebrants and servers would then walk through into the back of the cathedral and into the priests' sacristy.

Unlike all of the investigative journalists, I've walked that route. It's 308 steps. Now I'm a bit tall. So it's probably a bit more than 308 steps. But I've walked it with the man who was at the time the MC at the cathedral when the trial was going on. It takes 4 ½ minutes to do that walk.

We come to Pell in the record of interview. The allegations are put to him. He says, 'Now, the sacristy after mass is generally a hive of activity because you've – well have got the sacristan there and often you had an assistant sacristan. If there were concelebrants, they would divest. The servers would get out of their vestments. The collectors would bring in the collection. The sacristan and the assistants would be bringing the chalice and the vessels out from the altar. Now, I was always accompanied by my master of ceremonies after the mass, so he would come around with me and help me unrobe. It was just the protocol.[70]

When J's version was put to him, Pell said, 'What a load of absolute and disgraceful rubbish. Completely false. Madness. All sorts of people used to come to the sacristy to speak to the priest. The sacristans were around, and altar servers were around. This is the sacristy at the cathedral after Sunday Mass?' Mr Reed, the chief police investigator replied, 'yes'. To which Pell responded, 'Well, need I say anymore. What a load of garbage and falsehood and deranged falsehood. My master of ceremonies will be able to say that he was always with me after the ceremonies until we went back to the car park or back to the presbytery. The sacristan was around. The altar servers were around. People were coming and going.'[71]

At the trial the Chief Police investigator Mr Chris Reed was asked questions in light of what had been alleged in the priests' sacristy. He clarified that they didn't interview anyone who was a concelebrant; they didn't interview any money counters. There was an altar server by the name of Connor who had a diary. He was anally retentive. He kept a record of every mass and every server, and then the lunches they'd go to at Jimmy Watson's, and the servers who attended the lunches etc. The police had this diary. They did not interview one single altar server. They interviewed lots of choristers, but not a single altar server. When asked why not, the police investigator said, well the complainant said there were none there.

Now this is basic policing. Let's take an example which has nothing to do with victims of abuse. Let's say you have someone who says: 'I've witnessed a bank robbery and I was in the bank and I'm a pedestrian and this is what happened.' And the police say, 'Well we'd better interview another 30 pedestrians.' 'Did you interview any bank tellers?' 'No, because the pedestrian said she didn't see any.' But wouldn't you at least interview the bank tellers to try and find out what actually goes on inside the bank at the time it's alleged that the robbery occurred? No altar servers were interviewed.

---

[70] George Pell, Record of Interview, Rome, 19 October 2016, p. 171
[71] George Pell, Record of Interview, Rome, 19 October 2016, p. 138

It got worse. The prosecutor Mark Gibson QC was a very honourable man and I think a good barrister. He before the jury said, 'Well look, we've got to find the six minutes when there's no one in the sacristy.' So he said we need that six or seven minutes where there's no one else in the sacristy. He said to the jury what happened was the seven altar servers (at the head of the procession) adjourned to 'the utility room' for seven minutes. He had to correct that. There was no evidence of that. So basically the prosecution case to the jury was that for that 7 minutes, the altar servers simply disappeared. They weren't to be found anywhere. Now you who know how a solemn mass works, answer this: how would seven altar servers at that point, they come in, they bow to the crucifix, and then disappear for seven minutes? Where do they go? What do they do?[72]

The next issue that Pell highlighted was that it was an external procession. Now this is the complete giveaway of the case. Basic policing should have put an end to things at this stage. You see, in the early stages of investigation, the complainant told the police that he and his friend at the end of mass did what they always did: they made an internal procession from beside the sanctuary into the priests' sacristy - a mere 56 steps. This route made it almost comprehensible that yes we were doing the usual 56 steps in the internal possession, and we started fossicking around, and we found a bottle of wine in the priests'

---

[72]   By the time this aspect of the case got to the High Court, Ms K Judd, the DPP, took the extraordinary step of throwing her own prosecutor under the bus. Ms JUDD: There was evidence that they left that room. There was evidence of McGlone that they went to what they called the "worker sacristy" to unrobe. That was a different sacristy. That was the workers' room or the candle room. Let me take you to McGlone. BELL J: Is this going back to the position that the prosecution disavowed at trial? Ms JUDD: He incorrectly disavowed that there was no evidence, he was very generous in that. BRET WALKER SC IN REPLY: 'There was objection at trial on the basis of there being no evidentiary foundation for that argument and the Crown accepted the propriety of the objection and to the jury withdrew it. That is now, startlingly, to us, described as an incorrect disavowal by a very generous prosecutor of that theory. What we do not have, of course, is the second shoe dropping; so where is the evidence, the nonexistence of which, as understood by counsel on both sides at trial, led to the withdrawal by the prosecutor of such an argument and your Honours do not have it. In our submission, we should not have to deal with that kind of improvisation at this point. You will not find it in the exchange of written submissions, for example.'

sacristy, and as the two appeal court judges in the Victorian Court of Appeal (Ferguson and Maxwell) said: 'In the 2016 walk through' which the complainant did being filmed, J 'said that the choir would come up and down the internal sacristy corridor every Sunday, before and after mass.'[73] So it was as simple as that. That's what we always do; that's what he remembered. Pell in the record of interview in 2016 says, 'No that's not what we do; this is a solemn mass in Saint Patrick's Cathedral; we do an external procession'. And the senior investigator Sheridan bought in and says 'Really?' So Pell said, 'Yes go back to Melbourne and check it out'.

So they come back to Melbourne, and sure enough the police satisfy themselves that it probably was an external procession. So the next time we hear from J is when he turns up at the committal proceedings and he says, yes actually it was an external procession. We came down here, up here, along here, and processing along this way but by the time we got to about the South transept here, I and my mate spontaneously decided to split off from the procession and we decided to come inside, and then if you like resume the old route of the internal possession. Now that was 277 steps. OK, by the time it got to trial and he was quizzed before the jury, there was a problem. If he'd peeled off near the South transept, you've got a choir of 50 persons. He and his mate were both altos, so they were at the front of the procession. There are 40 or 50 choristers behind him, including adults, some of whom were men whose own sons were in the choir. The question was: 'Well surely you'd be seen, and this is a breach of discipline? You there at the school on a scholarship. You wouldn't be doing this sort of thing.' So by the time it comes to trial and it goes before the jury, J says, 'Oh no, we didn't come off at the southern transept; we kept going all the way to the toilet corridor, and then spontaneously without speaking to each other, we turned around and we retraced our steps down here into the South transept and into the priests' sacristy.' That's 408 steps. Just bear in mind: it takes 5 ½ minutes. OK, that's all you need to remember at this stage.

---

[73] Ferguson CJ and Maxwell P, *George Pell v The Queen* [2019] VSCA 186, #218

Pell for his part says, 'Well actually I wouldn't be anywhere around there because I'd come out on to the steps (at the West Door) and I'd be greeting people on the steps.' The prosecution conceded that Pell ultimately set up a protocol that he would always be greeting people on the steps unless he had business to run off to. But the prosecution claimed that with these first two solemn masses of a new Archbishop in the cathedral, he wouldn't have stayed there very long. Now you've got to say it's a bit counterintuitive, isn't it? I mean, if you're one given to standing on the cathedral steps, you as the new Archbishop at your first two masses: chances are you'd spend more rather than less time meeting your new parishioners. Even if you tried to get away, if you've ever met any of those anxious parishioners who are very keen to meet the new priest or the new Bishop. You think: 'Hey, George back here! We want to meet you.'

Now if in any doubt about what Pell's approach to things was then when he had just become the Archbishop: the Melbourne *Age* did a two-page spread on him: *The gospel according to Pell* at that time and they described him attending a Chinese priest's funeral:

> After the service they spill on to the concrete outside and the older
> Italians line up in front of Pell to pay their respects. They reach for
> his hand, then bend and kiss his knuckles or his ring in an ancient
> gesture of homage. Some wipe away tears. Pell is unsurprised
> and responds to each one with a few words or a blessing. Later,
> when he tries to pose for a photograph, he is surrounded by a flock
> of giggling nonnas half his size who want to get in the picture too.
> They are quite unembarrassed; he is their archbishop, the face of
> their church, and he belongs to them. This is Catholic faith in the
> old style, ritualised, tribalised and unquestioning.[74]

It's there on the cathedral steps: ritualized tribalized and unquestioning. And it takes time.

The next thing Pell says in his record of interview is: 'Look hang on,

---

[74] Karen Kissane, 'The Gospel According to George', *The Age*, Saturday Extra, 30 November 1996

142

this is a very solemn event. I'm there with my MC Monsignor Portelli. He's always with me in this sort of thing. And so once again the prosecutor doing a painstaking job tries to get Portelli out of the picture. This was another one of those 'A-ha' moments for me as a lawyer attending the proceedings. As you know, there were two trials because in the first trial, the jury couldn't agree. Gibson had to separate Pell and Portelli with evidence which was in some way coherent. So he said, 'Well maybe there was some event on in the cathedral that afternoon which meant that Portelli had to go and fix up the books in the sanctuary so he would be away for a couple of minutes.' The only event that afternoon on either day was the evening 5.30 mass. Now a suggestion was put to the jury that maybe Pell stayed and did that mass. There was no evidence of that. Why is there no evidence of it? Because as all of you know, if the Archbishop does the solemn mass at 11:00 AM, he doesn't traipse back to do the low mass at 5:30 on a Sunday afternoon.

But the real giveaway was this. Gibson at both trials says to Portelli: 'You're a smoker, aren't you? So maybe while you were fully vested, you just whipped out the back and had a smoke, so you're away for six or seven minutes.' He put that to the jury at the first trial and had to retract it before the jury. He did it again at the second trial. Now this fellow is a QC and is a very honourable man. He's a good lawyer. How does he twice make that mistake? He is so desperate to find that six or seven minutes to separate Pell from Portelli, and he had to retract yet again.

We then come to the magical 6 minutes – 6 minutes when Pell and the two boys are said to be there in the sacristy. The sacristan was man by the name of Potter in his 80s and by the time of the second trial, he was starting to lose it. Anyone who attended both trials knows that the great weight which was put by the DPP in the High Court and by the two appeal judges in Victoria of the majority on the six minutes was preposterous. Why? Because in the first trial there was no mention of 6 minutes private prayer time by Potter. But he did mention it in the second trial. So let me give you exactly the question and answer that was put to him:

> MR GIBSON: Mr Potter, can I ask this question. Once mass finishes and the procession commences down the nave towards the western door, once mass finishes and the procession commences how long is it before you first attend the sanctuary to start doing what you've just told us?

> MR POTTER: Could be five minutes. I make sure that the procession's cleared from the cathedral first. That the whole procession's moved through. And people will be walking up to the sanctuary area kneeling, so we didn't disturb them for that five or six minutes, we gave them their private time and then we would move in after that.[75]

In the Court of Appeal, Justices Maxwell and Ferguson: their key paragraph was paragraph 300 of their judgement. Listen to it. It is absurd:

> In our view, taking the evidence as a whole, it was open to the jury to find that the assaults took place in the 5-6 minutes of private prayer time and that this was before the 'hive of activity' described by the other witnesses began. The jury were not bound to have a reasonable doubt.[76]

So the offending occurred in the five or six minutes after the first servers step down the nave. And we know it takes the first servers 4 ½ minutes to get to the priests' sacristy. So 4 ½ of your 6 minutes have gone before even the first server gets there. We know according to J's

---

[75] Transcript, *The Queen* v *Pell*, 19 November 2018, p. 473.

[76] *George Pell* v *The Queen* [2019] VSCA 186, #300 [The Victorian Court of Appeal decision has not been reported in the authorised *Victorian Reports*]. In the Court of Appeal, Chief Justice Ferguson (who joined with President Maxwell in the majority, Justice Weinberg dissenting) made very few interventions during the course of oral argument. She largely confined herself to routine directions and to some observations about the vestments worn by Cardinal Pell. Her most substantive intervention was this observation offered to counsel for the DPP: 'Mr Boyce, the underlying theme perhaps not expressed in this way by you though, is really what you're saying is that the complainant's evidence was so strong, was so forceful, so credible, such that he was a witness of truth, beyond what you might see in other cases, that it's going to take a lot to create a reasonable doubt.'(Transcript, *George Pell* v *The Queen*, Court of Appeal, 6 June 2019, p. 212) That sentence is as neat a summary as you will find of her reasoning and that of Maxwell P in their very flawed judgment which was struck down 7-0 by the High Court.

evidence that 5 ½ minutes elapse before he and his mate travel their elaborate route. So in those six minutes, not even J and his mate are in the room. Meanwhile Pell is at the back of the procession. Even if he stayed on the steps for only 10 seconds, he is still not going to be there within 6 minutes. It's absolutely impossible.

If you want to know how bad the criminal justice system of Victoria has become, just consider this exchange in the High Court of Australia where the DPP herself appeared before all seven judges of the highest court in the land. She comes to the six minutes. She says: 'Well, I am really going to go in hard on this and say that six minutes is just not something that you can be definite about because what they say is that the period – there is a period of a quiet interlude. Now, how long that is and when it starts is very much dependent upon how long it takes for the cathedral to be cleared.'[77]

She went on to suggest that if there's a big congregation, it takes a long time for the cathedral to clear. That's not what Potter said in evidence. Potter never spoke about the clearing of the whole congregation from the cathedral. He spoke only about the clearing of the procession. He said the procession started at the foot of the sanctuary and that the private prayer time ran from when the first servers set off. He waits for the procession to clear before he does anything.

Chief Justice Kiefel asked the DPP: 'Ms Judd, was it put to any witness that it could be more than five to six minutes?' Judd fudges it, I won't read you the answer. The Chief Justice tries again: 'The question is not a difficult one, Ms Judd. Was it put to any witness that it could be more than five to six minutes?' She fudges her answer again. A touch exasperated the Chief Justice says, 'I take it the answer to my question is no?' Judd fudges again. The Chief Justice answers her own questions: 'But in the passages you have just taken us to, the prosecutor adopts the evidence of five to six minutes and goes with it.'[78]

---

[77]   *Pell* v *The Queen*, High Court Transcript, 12 March 2020, p. 52, available at http://www.austlii.edu.au/au/other/HCATrans/2020/27.html

[78]   Ibid, p. 55.

In the highest court of the land the most senior prosecutor of the state of Victoria invented a theory and then invented evidence. It's outrageous, and if in any doubt you can still watch the video of it on the High Court. Just observe the looks on the faces of the seven judges of the High Court of Australia wondering what in God's name is going on in Victoria!

Just to conclude. This was also against a background where Victoria police were up to no good and if you're in any doubt about that, just look at what happened at the time that there was the Victorian parliamentary inquiry. When Pell became the Archbishop in 1996, he negotiated a protocol with the Victoria police and the most senior Law Offices of Victoria. It remained in place from 1996 to 2011 – for 15 years. Then there was a Victorian parliamentary inquiry and the Victorian police fronted before that Victorian inquiry and said things which at the very least were not transparent. Let me simply quote what the Victorian inquiry said:

> It is clear that Victoria Police paid inadequate attention to the fundamental problems of the Melbourne Response arrangements until relatively recently in April 2012 and that, when they did become the subject of public attention, Victoria Police representatives endeavoured quite unfairly to distance the organisation from them.[79]

The delightful centrepiece of Mr Ashton appearing before that parliamentary inquiry was his bombshell revelation about 43 suicides related to clergy sexual abuse. He told the inquiry:

> Earlier this year we received a report from one of our detectives regarding work that was being pulled together on the issue of suicides as a result of clergy abuse. We have seen suicides as a result of clergy abuse. In relation to the material that was provided to us in a compiled format early this year, we met with the coroner and discussed the issues around those particular alleged suicides. I think there were 43 in number that were talked about at the broad level

---

[79] Parliament of Victoria, Family and Community Development Committee, Betrayal of Trust: Inquiry into the Handling of Child Abuse by Religious and other Non-Government Organisations, Volume 1, 2013, p. 25

that needed to be looked at. The coroner asked us to do a review of those individual cases to determine whether she should reopen any of those matters. We have now concluded that research, and we will be in a position very shortly — maybe in the next week or two — to go back to see the coroner and give her the results of that work.[80]

That then became a big national story and it helped fuel the call for a royal Commission. Within less than two weeks on 1 November 2012, the police received an intelligence brief from its Sexual Crimes Squad. I won't read it all to you. There's no time. But it turned out that of the 43 cases, '1 case had childhood sexual assault by a member of the clergy identified as a contributing factor in the motivations of the person for their death by suicide. There is no new evidence of fact or circumstances that would suggest that it is appropriate to re-open any of the investigations into the death of the nominated persons.'

So there it was: one case! And we were not told that until 2015. Be in no doubt: the police force had a job to do and it was to get Pell charged. The results were what Pell predicted.

So let me conclude by saying this: what we need for the good not just of people like Pell but also for the good of someone like J and for all *bona fide* complainants and victims and their supporters: we need good policing, good basic policing; we need honourable prosecution, and if in any doubt about our legal system, then in the end be grateful that we are part of a federation and we do have the High Court of Australia. I have my own criticisms to make of the High Court from time to time. I'm very critical of a judgment they gave on refugee issues this week where they split 4-3. But here 7-zip, where they said there's just nothing in this. So the big

lesson is: the media will continue with all sorts of intimation about Pell's guilt. There's no doubt that he's innocent. There's no doubt that he was made a scapegoat; and there is no doubt that the church does need the state to deal with these issues. But the state needs to act

---

[80] Victorian Parliament, Family and Community Development Committee, Hansard, 19 October 2012, p. 8.

honourably, and state officials need to do their job. When they don't, everybody suffers huge and lasting trauma. Mr J was put through two years of additional trauma where the most basic of policing would have put him out of his angst about all that he was then put through. These are the lessons for church and state from the Pell Saga. Thank you.

Q&A

This is with regards to the questionable manner in which the investigation took off advertising for complainants. Do you believe a royal Commission into the affair should be called?

There won't be any royal Commission in Victoria on this. They've already had a royal Commission. You might remember the Lawyer X inquiry. It's been a bit of déjà vu for me because I was brought up in Queensland in the early 70s when Joh Bjelke Peterson was the premier. A lot of what I've seen in Victoria is just a replay of what I saw in Queensland in the early 70s. Queensland was right of centre; Victoria is left of centre. They've had a Royal Commission there into Lawyer X where the royal commissioner found there are up to 1000 or more criminal convictions which are now questionable because of the appalling behaviour of the Victoria police in what they did with Lawyer X. The High Court of Australia once again unanimously labelled this as completely 'reprehensible' to which commissioner Ashton speaking to his favourite radio personality said, 'Oh yeah, well they've got their view'.

The Royal Commission then said there was a need to appoint an investigator. When that happened with the Fitzgerald inquiry in Queensland, the investigator was appointed before Fitzgerald finished his work. In Victoria, it's now over six months since that Royal Commission reported and there has been no investigator appointed.[81] Mind you, there are advertisements in the national newspapers to appoint a

---

[81] An investigator was appointed on 29 June 2021 but the legislation for the exercise of his functions has still not been passed as at 20 November 2021.

full time new judicial registrar of the Court of Appeal to deal just with the appeals of those who have been convicted with probably tainted evidence as a result of the activities of Victoria police and Lawyer X. So Victoria needs to implement its present Royal Commission. Getting to a Royal Commission on this one in addition to that, I think is all but inconceivable. Basically I think people have said, let the caravan move on. But I hope we would not see a repetition of that, and the way they advertised for people to come forward particularly on Christmas Eve in 2015. I thought was an absolute disgrace.

Was Mr. J coached by forces such as the police helping him to provide his evidence?

I don't know. I haven't seen the evidence Mr. J. I operate on the presumption that he was not, but I would have to say that I mean what you've seen there with the map where it changed from 56 steps to 277 steps to 408 steps. I mean clearly there was a lot going on. Let's just say that and I mean the absurdity of it was that J at least and the police having been convinced that it was an external procession. One problem was: how do we deal with an external procession and then still follow the path back for an internal procession from the southern transept to the priests' sacristy? But it created a whole new problem, namely that there just was not 6 minutes where Pell could be in the room and there wasn't six minutes when the two boys could be in the room, let alone 6 minutes when Pell and the two boys could be in the room alone together. It just can't be done, and if in any doubt, all I say to people nowadays is: let's forget about the evidence; just give us a theory; just give us a theory – any theory! It needs 6 minutes for them to be alone in the sacristy immediately after Mass. Give us a theory as to what happens with the altar servers. Give us the theory about all of this, and no one's come up with one.[82]

---

[82] In the High Court, Justice Bell put this very directly to the DPP who had absolutely no answer: 'On this theory of the case, between them bowing to the crucifix and going and changing, there is some five to six minutes in which the complainant and the other young man go into the room, they poke around, they swig the wine, the Archbishop comes in, there is the confrontation and

Is the Pell travesty a one off, or should we interpret it as an anti-Catholic bias in the Victorian government against Catholic institutions?

I don't think it's likely that we'll have the same concatenation of circumstances ever again where you've got all the horror of a Royal Commission; you've got someone like Pell who had become a lightning rod conductor, and you've got a desire by the Victorian police force to get a scalp. Now it may be that in the future there's those sorts of risks, but that's why I keep emphasising that we've got to maintain faith, but that faith has to be deserved in our key institutions particularly policing, particularly prosecutions, and particularly appeal courts. The mystery for me has always been that Mark Weinberg undoubtedly was the leading criminal appeal judge in the country and he was called back from retirement to sit on this case by the Chief Justice who was known (and it's no criticism of her) but it's known that criminal law was not her field. Now as I say if it were a tax case and you're the new Chief Justice and you don't know much about tax and you've got the leading tax lawyer of the country sitting beside you, you'd think you'd start by presuming that I'll be pretty attentive to what this tax lawyer has to say.

So whether that sort of thing would be repeated again, I would hope that particularly given the way the High Court judgment deals with these things, I would think some lessons have been learned. Just to give you one example. There's a paragraph in the High Court judgment when the DPP in her desperation wanted to get the matter back to Victoria rather than having the High Court decide it there and then. She submitted to them that they didn't have all the evidence available to make a decision, so no, why not refer it back to the Victorian Court of Appeal or maybe bring it back here again the High Court of Australia? Unanimously all seven judges quoted the submission and they said there is only one word to describe this submission: 'specious'. Now I know enough about how the High Court of Australia works to know that draft judgment sat on seven desks and each of them looked

---

the offence. All of that happening and the prosecution is unable to posit a theory of what the altar servers were doing.' Available at http://www.austlii.edu.au/au/other/HCATrans/2020/27.html

and said, 'Oh, specious. It's not a word we usually use. It's pretty strong stuff.' And each of them said, 'Yes, specious!' Now hopefully we can avoid that sort of thing.

I want to repeat again as I said I think during the proceedings the prosecutor through the trial Gibson I think was very honourable and did a very workmanlike job. He just did his job. But by the time it got to the High Court, you have the DPP in this exchange with Justice Virginia Bell: 'Is this going back to the position that the prosecution disavowed at trial?' Judd replied: 'He incorrectly disavowed that there was no evidence, he was very generous in that.' Judd just threw Gibson under the bus. You don't do that sort of thing in the High Court of Australia.

I did not think Lindy Chamberlain could be found guilty because there was no body and no motive. In the Pell case my balance left me. It was only after the High Court appeal and the publication of your book and the interview you gave that I could see rationality returning. Do you have any comment?

My only comment is this: what I've done in the book, it's just an accurate little book of reportage of every interview I gave and every article I wrote. They are there in chronological order. You might remember when I wrote that first article in *The Australian,* I copped quite a thrashing. I would still say going back and looking at that article today, I wouldn't change a word of it. In light of the High Court decision, I think a lot of people who were critical of me then might have cause to look again at what was being said. Now very deliberately, I decided that after the suppression order was lifted, I would write one and only one article and do three and only three interviews - two of the three were with the ABC: *7:30* and the *Drive* programme in Melbourne. I then made it clear I would not speak again until the legal processes had run their course. I thought it was not proper for someone like myself with a profile as I have to be buying into a public debate until everything had run its course in the courts.

When the High Court gave its decision, I then wrote three or four articles and I gave only one interview. I very deliberately did not give that interview to the ABC because I thought that the ABC by that time had not conducted itself in a dispassionate professional manner. I thought their calling me in at that stage as they wanted to would be simply the old game of restoring balance. Well I'm not in the game of hanging around just to restore balance when there's that sort of media reporting going on.

It's very necessary for us to be respectful of legal processes but then let's actually do the hard work of looking at the evidence and then identifying the problems that are there. I mean it is extraordinary in Australia at the moment: if it were a 4-3 or 5-2 decision of the High Court, you might say well maybe there's something in this. But that it's 7 zip and that it's written in the way that it is: it is very clear that the High Court was of the view that this was not a case which should have proceeded.

Cardinal Pell has received justice. Is it possible for J to receive justice?

The tragedy is we don't know what's happened to J. We do know this: there's no way that what he said occurred when and where he said – no way. It's just impossible. Given the changes of thinking that went on, there were obviously all sorts of mental processes at play. We do know from some of the records that he says that he suffered abuse when he was a young boy by someone who was childminding at his home. And he says he was abused by his parish priest when he was a young altar server. Now this is of course a whole other scenario. In terms of justice for J, what I've been arguing tonight is that justice for J would require us to ask what it means when the Prime Minister says in the apology, 'We believe you'. It means this: J, we respect you, and we will take on board absolutely everything you say, and we will do thoroughly professional police work and the prosecution will do thoroughly professional prosecution work determining whether your case should be pursued.

Now with quite a number of the Ballarat cases, that was done, and the cases were quite rightly thrown out. You might remember it was in the media at the time that there were allegations that Pell raped a child while watching a movie in the picture theatre. It was demonstrated that amongst other things the kid said he had a vivid memory of what movie was showing. The movie wasn't showing at that time, and the fellow who ran the movie theatre said that if this had been going on in his movie theatre, he would have known something about it. So justice for that person meant: 'Look, we don't know what happened in your life, but this is not a case to be prosecuted where there would be risks to everyone, yourself included.' I would say that justice for J would be with the sort of basic police work that should have been done after the record of interview of Pell, it should have been: 'This is not an appropriate case to go forward'.

The other thing to say is this: even the committing magistrate said, 'There was a preponderance of evidence that the archbishop spent time speaking with the congregants on the steps prior to returning to the sacristy. If a jury accepted the evidence of Monsignor Portelli and Mr Potter that the archbishop was never in the sacristy robed and alone, and that choirboys could never access the sacristy keys because they were always locked when unused, then a jury could not convict.'[83] Now a lot of people don't appreciate this. The prosecution because they were calling 23 witnesses, 22 of whom would have been those who worked around the church or whatever, the prosecution was given permission in relation to a number of them including Portelli and Potter that they would be allowed to cross examine them, basically to question their honesty or credibility or recall, even though they were their own witnesses, the prosecution witnesses. So the prosecution went to the trouble of getting that permission and never exercised it. Now you're left with a case where the committing magistrate says, 'If a jury accepted the evidence of Monsignor Portelli and Mr Potter … then a jury could not convict.' You've got permission to cross examine Portelli and Potter - to say: you know this is bunkum, and you don't take up the option.

[83] Ms B. Wallington, *The Police* v *George Pell*, Transcript, 1 May 2018, pp. 1786-7

That then leaves us and let's make no mistake for us as church and it's what I said in the 1st *7:30* interview the night after the lifting of the suppression order. The truly dreadful thing that we all have to accept as Catholics in contemporary Australia is that 12 presumably decent Aussies off the street sat through all this and said, 'We don't care. We're going to slot him.' I think you can see here tonight that on the available evidence, there's no way you could slot anyone on this unless there is a collective mindset that you know we want to slot this fellow for something, and we're slotting him for this.

What is the role of judges? On my understanding you get convicted in a criminal prosecution if it's proved beyond reasonable doubt. In a civil case, it's on the balance of probabilities. Does a judge have some duty to direct the jury? In a case like this you probably couldn't even satisfy the civil level that you know on the balance of probabilities does the judge have a role to play in saying this should not go ahead?

In some jurisdictions the judge does have a role but not in Victoria. In Victoria once the prosecution, and this is why the role of DPP is so important, once the prosecution is on foot, the judge is basically powerless other than just to let the thing run its course. Now we'll never know what Justice Kidd, the trial judge, thought. I always thought that his final charge to the jury was a very light touch sort of charge, and I came away thinking that he probably thinks this isn't going to go anywhere in terms of conviction. But I may be quite wrong on that. For example, he managed to do his final charge without even mentioning a mitre or a crozier. Well if Pell turns up in the priests' sacristy without a mitre or a crozier, that's actually evidence that he must have been out there on the steps because it's only if he leaves the procession and stays on the steps for a considerable period of time that he will hand over the mitre and the crozier. And the mitre bearer and the crozier bearer will go ahead. But those things were left untouched in the final charge. I might just quote what he said about the different routes. This will give you an idea of how light his touch was on all that. I'm not being critical of him. I'm just saying that it was a light touch final charge. This is what the trial judge said to the jury:

'It does seem common ground, however, between the parties, that there are some differences in [J's] accounts… In relation to the first episode concerning the priests' sacristy, at the committal Mr J drew a diagram on the cathedral plan showing the way he left the procession and veered off at the south transept into the doors. …[T]here is that line which shows veering off from the procession, not far from the south transept and into the south transept. At trial he said they went up to the toilet corridors near the iron gate and doubled back, so that is a difference. It seems common ground there is a difference there and both parties made arguments to you about what flows from that'.

I haven't even dealt tonight with the fifth charge which if you think these four charges were preposterous, the fifth charge was just interplanetary stuff. Pell was standing next to Father Brendan Egan who said the mass. At the end of the mass they're all in a corridor with probably 40 or 50 people there. Pell peels off, goes off in the midst of all these people, puts the kid against the wall, assaults him and then comes back and joins the procession. And guess what: the police to this day, to this day, have never spoken to Brendan Egan. Now he did leave the priesthood, but he's been working for a local council in Victoria readily contactable - and never spoken to by the police. And you put that charge against a citizen who happens to be George Pell – ridiculous!

There was a variety of opinions expressed in the politics and religion class of year 11 about Cardinal Pell's defence choice of lawyer, his refusing or choosing not to take the stand etc. What was your opinion?

I don't mind saying because it's not a claim made in hindsight, and to be fair and gracious Cardinal Pell acknowledges in his *Prison Journal* that after the first trial when he didn't give evidence I wrote to him telling him he must give evidence and I went to see him and I had a long talk with him and I fronted up for the second trial and I mean I wasn't part of Team Pell or whatever so I was in the dark as much as anyone.[84] It seemed to me that Richter was upping the ante a bit in the second trial and I thought that there was something going on here, but I thought that's OK because Pell's going to give evidence. This time, the first time my heart sank, was then at the end of the prosecution case, when it was announced that Pell was not giving evidence. There's a saying in the law, using an American term: we don't want Monday morning quarterbacks. After the game everyone's an expert and says what went wrong and that you should have done something different. I remain convinced, as I was between the first and second trial, that basically and I don't think the criminal lawyers had got this, I think they would in future. I mean criminal lawyers are very good at acting within the box but I think in this case it had reached the stage in the Australian public mind where I think ordinary decent jurors said we're sick to death of the Catholic Church spending big money to employ flash lawyers who cross examine the complainant for two days or whatever, and then this guy who's obviously very bright and all the rest of it doesn't even get in the box and eyeball us and tell us there's no way that could have happened.

Now I may well be wrong, but I think one of the lessons out of the Pell saga is that if there is a prominent church person in that sort of position in future then basically you've got to front the jurors; you've got to eyeball your fellow citizens, and you have to say, 'No, there is no way I could possibly have done what was alleged.'

The Pell case shows without a doubt that there is active discrimination in our institutions, namely police and judiciary, against Catholic clergy. Given this, what do you think would be the bare minimum that needs to be done with the federal Religious Discrimination Bill

---

[84] In Volume one of his *Prison Journal*, Cardinal Pell writes at page 64: 'Frank Brennan was always keen for me to be in the box, especially after the hung jury decision. Eventually I decided I should give evidence, despite the entire legal team and my own advisers being opposed. Terry Tobin came around to my point of view. I only decided not to take the stand after the prosecutor had dealt with Charlie Portelli and especially Max Potter. I was so cross with the treatment they both received, I was frightened that my hostility might turn a majority for acquittal into a split decision. The basis of my reasoning was quite wrong.'

or otherwise to ensure there is true religious liberty and true non-discrimination against people of faith in Australia? [by a Member of the House of Representatives]

I'll be happy to come and see you in your office sometime and talk about these things. I've always had a rule. I chaired the inquiry for the Rudd government on national human rights. I was then on the committee Turnbull set up on religious freedom chaired by Ruddock. I've had a rule for myself that if you work on a committee like that, you do your report, you put it in, and you let it speak for itself. So that's been my approach.

One reason I've had that approach is that years ago there was a judge of whom I thought very highly, Justice Lockhart. Now I disagreed with him on things to do with stem cell research and he did a major inquiry on stem cell research. I think he died or was unwell so some of the public servants and others who have been involved in the inquiry evangelised very strongly for it, and I just didn't think that was right. I think it's very appropriate for any member of parliament to seek my views about these things, but I don't think it's appropriate for me to be evangelising that cause.

But I will say this. I became convinced in 2009 that Australia does need something like an overarching Human Rights Act. But that is not the will of our major political parties at this stage. The track we've gone down in Australia is with a whole bevy of discrimination laws: racial discrimination, age discrimination etc. Given that that's the track we've gone down, I think there is a *prime face* case for having a religious discrimination law providing that you shouldn't discriminate against people on the basis of religion. But where it becomes highly problematic is this: with a Religious Discrimination Act you would need far more exemptions than you would in other sorts of discrimination laws. Why? Because religious people want to be able to choose people of their own religion for particular functions for very understandable reasons.

The thing about religion is that if I'm a Christian, I actually believe that Jesus Christ is the saviour. I actually believe that Christianity is the best religion. If I'm a Muslim, I don't believe Christianity is the best religion. I believe Islam is the best religion. Now in that sort of situation, I think the work to be done by a discrimination law is very different from what it is in things like race discrimination and age discrimination. So there are many complexities in all of that. Having said that, I think what's essential is to ensure that within our public institutions that there is no discrimination including religious discrimination and it would be absolutely appalling if there were ongoing discrimination against Catholics by a particular state police force. I think it's no secret that I mean clearly there was an antipathy or a strong difference between George Pell as a leading Catholic and Graham Ashton as the Victorian police commissioner. But hopefully we can all move on from the sorts of abuse which occurred during the Pell proceedings.

I think the jury did want Pell to be responsible for child sex offences within the church. I agree that Pell in the criminal sense is not guilty but who in the church will take responsibility for the abhorrent treatment of children. Until responsibility is taken, the church has a problem with the public.

I readily concede that and that's why I started with the quotes from Cardinal Marx and from Pope Francis. In Pell's defence and in the church's defence, I would say this: I think the Royal Commission did a lot of good work but where I think the follow up on the Royal Commission has not been good is I think there was insufficient acknowledgment that the Catholic Church had done a lot of work since 1996 to get its house in order. There were still failures but there was a lot of work that was done in order to get that house in order. Part of the problem has been that where you have particularly some in the media saying that the Catholic Church is a complete cot case, while there are people in the church who have sweated long and hard between 1996 and 2021 – which is 25 years – who feel how can we ever get it right? Definitely some of those people would simply say: well the sooner the Catholic Church goes away, the better. As we know, the Catholic Church isn't going to go away. But what we do want to ensure is that we do have the appropriate accountabilities.

I've heard that there was a story very similar to the complainant's account in America some years ago.

I don't know anything about it so I'm not in a position to believe it or not believe it.

Could you comment on the allegations and suggestions about Vatican finances being used to get Pell in this case?

I think this has been one of the very unfortunate things. If there had been better policing, better prosecution, and better work by the Victorian Court of Appeal, we would all be spared these conspiracy theories about Vatican money and witness J. Who knows? I would still be very surprised and on all of these things I say: 'Let's wait and see the evidence'. And that's exactly what I tried to do during the course of the Pell trials. Let's see the evidence, and let's apply the appropriate standard of proof. Now for my money, anything else simply remains surmise or conspiracy theories.

I remember once, and I don't think he'd mind my saying this: Cardinal Pell spoke to me about some of the intrigues going on in the Vatican and I said to him, 'Look all these years I have taken no notice whatever of these intrigues in the Vatican. It would simply be a threat to my faith.' He said to me, 'Someone like yourself should be interested and should be involved.' But to this day, I find that I have more than enough things to interest me and more than enough things to do without trying to get on top of the intrigues of Vatican finances.

Joanne Gale's Vote of Thanks

It might bring me bad luck to quote a saint other than Thomas More at the Thomas More Forum but I'm going to do it anyway. In the words of Saint Ambrose, no duty is more urgent than returning thanks. And so it's my privilege to say a few words of thanks on behalf of the Thomas More Parish. My name is Joanne. I'm a member of the parish council and my legal expertise consists of watching British police dramas. I was pleasantly surprised that I could follow Fr Frank's presentation, and I suspect this is due to his talent for explaining complex processes and issues in such a way that even consumers of low brow television such as myself can understand. Father Frank's presence at the trials, his scrutiny of the court transcripts and evidence, and his presentations of his findings in the media, in his book, and here with us tonight give all of us an important opportunity to deepen our knowledge and understanding of this very complex chapter in the Australian Catholic Church, indeed in Australian history. He has thoughtfully and carefully presented his analysis always with empathy for the parties involved. From the start of this whole episode, he's being a consistent and constant voice asking for people to examine the facts: in the context, a very courageous stance. Father Frank's calls for truth, justice and healing echoed loud and clear.

My husband Ross and I live in a household with two boys under the age of four and therefore spend a shockingly disproportionate amount of time talking about superheroes. Superheroes are seekers of truth and justice, and above all they're compassionate and courageous. Now while Father Frank might not wear his undergarments on the outside of his clothing, he comes pretty close to a superhero classification in our household. Father Frank as a Catholic community gathered here this evening, we're all very grateful for your efforts to seek truth and justice for all involved, including the church. We thank you for writing the book so that we may learn from your insights and we thank you for your generosity in sharing your journey here with us tonight. We've got a small token for you on behalf of the parish.

18

The Anatomy of a Vendetta

Catholic Weekly

5 September 2021

It's time to declare that George Pell is innocent of the preposterous charges he faced in the County Court of Victoria and to move on for the good of everyone, including bona fide complainants and victims of child sexual abuse in institutions.

Because of the suppression orders put in place by the County Court, you were unable to follow the trials of Cardinal George Pell day by day. That's why I was asked to attend the proceedings. That's why I have published this book, *Observations on the Pell Proceedings* – so you can make your own assessment of the evidence.

My book is dedicated 'to those who seek truth, justice and healing and to those who have been denied them'. Having followed the Pell proceedings closely, I am convinced that the case did nothing to help bona fide complainants, victims, and their supporters. I write in the introduction: 'The failures of the Victoria police, prosecution authorities, and the two most senior Victorian judges in these proceedings did nothing to help the efforts being made to address the trauma of institutional child sexual abuse. As a society we need to do better, and the legal system needs to play its part.' I am convinced that light and healing can be more readily sought and hoped for if appropriate steps are taken to correct the errors made in the Pell proceedings. The compounding errors resulted in the unanimous judgment of the High Court of Australia which placed the Victorian criminal justice system in a very poor light.

I was left in no doubt. Cardinal Pell was innocent of these charges. He should never have even been charged.

At the first trial, the jury could not agree. So a second trial was held at which Pell was convicted of all five charges. The Victorian Court of Appeal upheld the convictions by 2-1. The dissenting judge was Mark Weinberg, the most experienced criminal appeal court judge in the country. He has now completely retired from the bench having taken up the demanding task of Special Investigator into the Afghanistan war crime allegations. The High Court sat all seven judges on the final appeal. They were unanimous in their judgment signing on to just one statement of reasons ordering that Pell's 'convictions be quashed and judgments of acquittal be entered in their place.'

At trial, the defence called no evidence. The prosecution main witness was the complainant 'J' (his name was and remains suppressed) who described what he said he recalled having happened to him and his friend the now deceased 'R' in 1996 when they were 13 years of age. But the prosecution also called, at the request of the defence, a lot of other witnesses who were involved with the solemn masses celebrated in St Patrick's Cathedral Melbourne in late 1996 – sacristan, MC, choristers, choir master and organist. Given that it was alleged that four of the five offences were said to have occurred in the priests' sacristy shortly after mass when usually you expect to find altar servers in attendance, it was surprising that the police did not interview any altar servers and the prosecution was not minded to call any altar servers until the defence forced their hand. By the time of the second trial, two altar servers recommended for inclusion by the defence were called by the prosecution to give evidence. One of these altar servers, Jeff Connor, had a comprehensive diary which allowed the prosecution to identify the only possible dates for the offences to have occurred: 15 and 22 December 1996. The other altar server, Daniel McGlone who is now a barrister, provided evidence of his attendance at one of these masses where he and his mother met Archbishop Pell on the steps after mass.

The High Court noted: 'The trial judge held that evidence adduced by the prosecution that was inconsistent with, or likely to contradict, J's account of events, was relevantly "unfavourable". His Honour granted leave to the prosecutor to cross-examine a number of witnesses (and foreshadowed the grant of leave in relation to other witnesses)' with respect to six topics.[85]

Despite having obtained the leave to cross-examine, the prosecution never took up that option and so never challenged the version of events given by the opportunity witnesses.

The six topics included: '(i) whether (Pell) was always in the company of another, including (the MC) Portelli or (the sacristan) Potter, when robed; (ii) whether (Pell) always greeted congregants on the steps of the Cathedral following Sunday solemn Mass'. The High Court noted that this grant of leave to cross-examine 'reflected the trial judge's satisfaction that the anticipated evidence, if accepted, excluded the realistic possibility of the offending having occurred as J described it.'[86]

The High Court noted, 'The honesty of the opportunity witnesses was not in question.'[87]

In its conclusion, the High Court realising that the crown case was full of holes decided to focus on just a few essentials. The court saw no need to address all the improbabilities or impossibilities raised by the defence. The court said: 'The likelihood of two choirboys in their gowns being able to slip away from the procession without detection; of finding altar wine in an unlocked cupboard; and of the applicant being able to manoeuvre his vestments to expose his penis are considerations that may be put to one side.'[88] There was no need

---

[85] *Pell* v *The Queen* (2020) 258 *Commonwealth Law Reports* 123, 142.
[86] *Pell* v *The Queen* (2020) 258 CLR 123, 142.
[87] *Pell* v *The Queen* (2020) 258 CLR 123, 160.
[88] *Pell* v *The Queen* (2020) 258 CLR 123, 164.

to consider the possibility or likelihood of these matters.

Having reviewed all the evidence and having accepted for the purposes of argument that 'the Court of Appeal majority did not err in holding that J's evidence of the first incident did not contain discrepancies, or display inadequacies, of such a character as to require the jury to have entertained a doubt as to guilt', the Court went on to conclude:

> 'It remains that the evidence of witnesses, whose honesty was not in question, (i) placed (Pell) on the steps of the Cathedral for at least ten minutes after Mass on 15 and 22 December 1996; (ii) placed him in the company of Portelli when he returned to the priests' sacristy to remove his vestments; and (iii) described continuous traffic into and out of the priests' sacristy for ten to 15 minutes after the altar servers completed their bows to the crucifix.'[89]

So that was it – game, set and match. On the evidence led in the case, there was no way that Pell and the two boys could have been alone together in the priests' sacristy soon after mass. There was neither time nor place for the offences to be committed. Absent both time and place in any narrative and you are in the realm of fantasy or false memory. The most basic police work would have disclosed this early in an investigation, particularly in a properly run investigation which had the huge resources committed as the Victoria Police dedicated to Operation Tethering which had Pell as its sole focus.

When the complainant J first presented to police on 18 June 2015, he had a fairly simple account of how he, his friend R and Cardinal Pell came to be in the priests' sacristy at St Patricks Cathedral on their own while Pell did dreadful things to them. They were finishing mass, and as usual, they were in an internal procession going directly from the sanctuary to the choir room via a corridor which passed the priests' sacristy which they had never previously entered. They would have taken only 56 steps to get there. The two boys started ferreting around going to places they should not go, and they discovered some altar wine in the priests' sacristy and started swilling it. Mind you,

---

[89]   *Pell* v *The Queen* (2020) 258 CLR 123, 168.

even this account was problematic. Where were all the other people who would be passing along that corridor at that time, and especially, where were the people who would have been coming and going from the priests' sacristy immediately after mass, ferrying things from the sanctuary, bringing in money for collection or counting, concelebrants changing out of their garb etc? J stated that he never revisited the priests' sacristy until the police took him on a walk through preparing for the case.

If the journalist Louise Milligan were accurate in her reporting and if R's mother was rightly recalling her own conversation with J, J also had another account at that time. Let me quote Milligan's account directly which purports to be a record of the conversation between Milligan and the mother 'sometime after the detectives took her statement' on 1 July 2015, which was after J had provided his first statement to police on 18 June 2015 (but before he made his second statement on 31 July 2015) alleging that the offending had occurred after mass:

> "(J) gently told her what he says happened with the Archbishop. 'He told me that himself and [my son] used to play in the back of the Church in the closed-off rooms,' she says.
>
> 'In the cathedral?' I ask her.
>
> 'In the cathedral, yep. And um, they got sprung by Archbishop Pell and he locked the door and he made them perform oral sex.' (J) still remembered the incident so clearly. Being picked up afterwards by his parents. Staring out the car window on the way home."[90]

In the second edition of her book *Cardinal*, Milligan changed the detail about a locked door to a blocked door, and omitted all reference to J being picked up by his parents. The effect of these changes was

---

[90] Louise Milligan, *The Cardinal*, Melbourne University Press, 1st edition, 2017, p. 352. In her second edition, Milligan adds: 'It has since been shown that what The Kid said is that Pell blocked, not locked, the door.' Without any explanation, she omits all reference to Mrs R telling Milligan that J had told her that he and R had been picked up by J's parents after the incident. At trial J could not remember whether he'd been picked up by one or both of his parents or by Mrs R herself or Mr R or both of them.

to bring her account more into line with the evidence J gave at trial. Milligan doesn't explain whether the other boy's mother just got these things wrong or whether Milligan got them wrong. But it doesn't much matter.

This second account of recurring ferreting in back rooms when no one else was around was dropped altogether, or more accurately never adopted by the prosecution. Milligan didn't give it much more of a run. It became generally known that Pell did not live at the cathedral presbytery and was only ever there for major liturgical events.

The first account of a one-off escapade straight after mass received a considerable re-working.

You will recall that Shane Patton (who when appointed Victorian Police Commissioner in June 2020 was described as 'forthright and analytical', with his colleagues saying he was 'right into the detail'[91]) led a couple of his men to Rome to interview Cardinal Pell on 19 October 2016. At the interview, Detective Sergeant Chris Reed was accompanied by Detective Inspector Paul Sheridan.

Preparing for the record of interview, Pell had thought, in light of the preliminary written details given him by the police, that the allegations related to assaults in a back room of the cathedral some time after choir practice when others would not be around – much like the Milligan account which was published a year later. But it was now made clear to him that the allegation was that the assaults occurred soon after solemn 11am mass in the priests' sacristy. Having heard that, Pell must have thought that the police would realise that J's allegations were unreliable, if not ridiculous.

At the outset in the interview Pell told the police: 'The allegations relating to Saint Patrick's cathedral are ...the products of fantasy.' He went on to say:

> 'The most rudimentary interview of staff and those who were choir

---

91 See https://www.theage.com.au/national/victoria/victoria-s-new-po-lice-chief-commissioner-announced-20200601-p54ycv.html

boys at the cathedral in that year and later would confirm that the allegations are fundamentally improbable and most certainly false and I invite my interviewers to tell me who they've spoken to and I'm happy to provide them in due course the persons who can speak authoritatively about my functions, presence and conduct at the cathedral generally and more particularly at times when abuse is alleged to have occurred. I would earnestly hope that this is done before any decision is made whether to lay charges because immeasurable damage will be done to me and to the church by the mere laying of charges which on proper examination will later be found to be untrue. Thank you.'[92]

Detective Sergeant Chris Reed responded, 'Thank you. I appreciate that.' Mr Reed, Mr Patton, and Detective Superintendent Sheridan returned to Australia and did nothing of the sort. Pell gave the police four vital pieces of information of which they were previously unaware, and which should have brought the investigation to an end after some very simple police work back home.

FOUR VITAL PIECES OF INFORMATION FROM THE PELL RECORD OF INTERVIEW, 19 October 2016

1. The Hive of Activity in the Priests' Sacristy After Mass

The first vital piece of information was that there would be a hive of activity in the priests' sacristy after mass, including the sacristan, his assistant, money collectors, concelebrants and altar servers. Pell told the police that they should go back to Melbourne and interview these people who would be able to corroborate his claim that it was just not possible for Pell to be alone in that place at that time with two choir boys. Here are Pell's actual words spoken at the record of interview:

Now, the sacristy after mass is generally a hive of activity because you've, well have got the sacristan there and often you had an assistant sacristan. If there were concelebrants, they would divest. The servers

---

[92]   George Pell, Record of Interview, Rome, 19 October 2016, pp. 9-10

would get out of their vestments. The collectors would bring in the collection. The sacristan and the assistants would be bringing the chalice and the vessels out from the altar. Now, I was always accompanied by my master of ceremonies after the mass, so he would come around with me and help me unrobe. It was just the protocol.[93]

When J's version was put to him, Pell said, 'What a load of absolute and disgraceful rubbish. Completely false. Madness. All sorts of people used to come to the sacristy to speak to the priest. The sacristans were around, and altar servers were around. This is the sacristy at the cathedral after Sunday Mass?' Mr Reed replied, 'yes'. To which Pell responded, 'Well, need I say anymore. What a load of garbage and falsehood and deranged falsehood. My master of ceremonies will be able to say that he was always with me after the ceremonies until we went back to the car park or back to the presbytery. The sacristan was around. The altar servers were around. People were coming and going.'[94]

The police led by Mr Patton with an eye for detail returned to Melbourne and did not interview one single money collector nor one single altar server. By the time of the second trial, the police had been provided with the diary of an altar server Jeff Connor who documented key participants at each mass. Here is Robert Richter's cross examination of Christopher Reed the lead investigator at trial:

> Yes. One of the interesting things about his diary is you were able to establish, from his diary, the names of a whole lot of altar servers, who were relevant to the relevant period?
>
> ---Well, relevant period. There was altar servers - I don't - I actually don't recall reading the - a name of altar servers in the diary of Mr Connor.
>
> Well, in the diary entries he has lunch, they have regular lunches?
>
> ---Okay.

---

[93] George Pell, Record of Interview, Rome, 19 October 2016, p. 171.
[94] George Pell, Record of Interview, Rome, 19 October 2016, p. 138.

Do you recall reading something like that, and he names them? For example, in July, 'Serves luncheon at Jimmy Watson's Lygon Street, Carlton, with Ray, Ralph' and a few other names there that I can't read?

---I don't recall that entry, no.

All right. They had regular lunches, get togethers, the altar servers, the adults?

---Okay.

You accept that, don't you?

---Yes, I'll accept that, yes.

So what happens is this; apart from the fact that we tracked down Mr Connor you had not tracked down any altar servers at all?

---No, that's correct.

But the altar servers were a very, very important part of this investigation?

---Well, not during the investigative stage, no, we were concerned with the choir boys specifically, because the events that have been alleged occurred surrounding the choir boys, not the altar servers that were in a different location and had a different role.

But there weren't any choir boys present when this happened, alleged to have happened?

---Well, there weren't any altar servers.

There weren't any of those present - - -?

---There weren't any altar servers alleged to be present either.

Correct, but the altar servers took part in processions in the same way that the choir boys took part in the processions?

---That's correct, yes.

And not just that, the altar boys were more important because the altar boys were in a position to say what they did after mass in the priest sacristy?

---Evidence has been given to that effect, yes.

Yes, and you accept that?

---I accept the evidence that's given, yeah.

So the situation is that apart from Jeff Connor - it was certainly possible to ask him for the names of other altar servers who were operational at the time?

---Yes, it was.

But he was never asked by anyone in the taskforce?

---No, he wasn't.[95]

No attempt was made by the police on their return from Rome to contact any altar server, or any money collector, or any concelebrant. Why? Because J said none of them was in attendance. Pell had told them that these people would routinely have been in attendance in the very spot and at the very time that the offending was alleged to have occurred. Instead of investigating the allegations, the police simply accepted J's account unquestioningly including the assertion that there were no altar servers present during any of the periods that the first incident could have occurred. They interviewed no altar servers. But they interviewed over 30 choristers. Why? Because J was a chorister. Choristers don't enter the priests' sacristy after mass, unless of course they are misbehaving.

This policing technique, if applied to other cases, would compromise many a criminal investigation. Let's consider an example where police receive a report of a crime, not from a victim but from someone who is simply an honest eyewitness. Imagine if a pedestrian claimed to witness a bank robbery, telling the police that she did not see any bank tellers in attendance when the bank vault was raided. The police then spend 18 months interviewing 30 other pedestrians, but they decide not to interview any bank tellers because the pedestrian witness said she did not see any. The police would want to interview all avail-

---

[95] *Director of Public Prosecutions v. George Pell,* Transcript of Proceedings, pp. 1268-1270, 29 November 2018

able bank tellers if only to learn from them what their usual practices were, assisting the police to understand how the robbery could possibly have happened. The necessity of interviewing the bank tellers as part of a proper investigation is underscored if there is evidence that routinely bank tellers would be in attendance at the time the robbery occurred.

2. The Procession Route (see diagram on page 82)

During the record of interview, Pell told the police that it was usual after a solemn mass in the cathedral celebrated by the archbishop that the whole entourage including the choir of up to 60 members would not recess simply by way of an internal procession of 56 steps from the sanctuary direct to the sacristy. Rather with the full fanfare of a recessional hymn followed by an Organ Voluntary, they would all process down the central nave exiting at the west door, then engaging in an external procession around the south side of the cathedral. I've measured that route at 308 steps. Together with the cathedral MC I have walked the route at procession speed. It takes about 4 ½ minutes. I should note that being over 6' 4", my steps tend to more than average.

Pell told the police to go back to Melbourne and speak to the relevant people. When they got back to Melbourne the police found that cathedral personnel like the MC Monsignor Charles Portelli, the choirmaster Mr John Mallinson, the organist Dr Geoff Cox, and the sacristan Mr Max Potter confirmed what Pell had said about external processions. If the weather were inclement or if Pell had another appointment shortly after mass, they would do an internal procession. But otherwise they would process externally. There would be lots of tourists around. It was obviously something of a spectacle. J seemed to be on his own, claiming that internal processions were routine and the order of the day.

By the time of the committal proceedings in March 2018, J's evidence was that on the day of the first four offences there had indeed been an external procession, and not an internal procession as he had earlier claimed in his police statements of 18 June 2015 and 31 July 2015 and in his later walk-through with the police on 29 March 2016 at the cathedral. Victorian Supreme Court Justices Chief Justice Ferguson and President Maxwell wrote in their judgment: 'In the 2016 walk-through, J said that the choir would come up and down the internal sacristy corridor every Sunday, before and after Mass.'[96] For some unexplained reason, J remained fixed on the idea that he and R gained access to the priests' sacristy via the corridor they would have used if it had still been an internal procession. He described a two step route. First there was an external procession. Second, when he and R got close to the south transept, the two of them without any prior planning and without any discussion peeled off from the procession, entering the cathedral via one of the doors at the south transept, then following the corridor which they would have taken if it were an internal procession. I have measured that route. It is 277 steps.

By the time Pell came to his first trial in the County Court in August 2018, J was confronted with a mountain of evidence from other witnesses called by the prosecution who claimed that it would be very difficult for two young boy sopranos at the front of the procession to peel off from the procession while it was still in train outside the cathedral, and to do so without being seen by others including adult choir members who would have been in line behind them with a clear line of sight. Later, J's evidence became that he and R had remained in the procession until it reached the toilet corridor hidden from the view of the tourists. The toilet corridor is a narrow passageway outside the cathedral that provides access to public toilets and to the sacristies via a locked door. J and another chorister Andrew La Greca (on whom Louise Milligan was very reliant[97]) gave evidence that by

---

96   *George Pell* v *The Queen* [2019] VSCA 186, #218

97   Andrew La Greca featured prominently in Louise Milligan's ABC *4 Corners* program 'The Conviction of Cardinal Pell', 4 March 1989. She interviewed him on air for 4 minutes, longer than any other person interviewed. The other persons interviewed at length were the retired policeman Doug Smith and Les Tyack who saw Pell in a change shed at Torquay in the mid-1980s. See https://www.abc.net.au/4corners/guilty:-the-conviction-of-cardinal-pell/10869116.

the time the procession reached the toilet corridor, order was breaking down and people were starting to disperse. So while inside the toilet corridor which is just 1.33m wide, J and R spontaneously and without any prior planning or discussion decided to go against the flow, finding their way out of the toilet corridor, back to the south transept then resuming the route which they would have taken to the priests' sacristy if indeed it had been an internal procession. He insisted that they walked; they did not run. I have measured this new convoluted route at 408 steps. It takes 5 ½ minutes.

By the time of the second trial, the prosecution, searching to find the 6 minutes during which the offending was said to have occurred, had postulated that the offending must have occurred during the private prayer time after mass. This 6 minutes was said to be the time that the sacristan Max Potter allowed for congregants to pray uninterrupted after mass before he got his altar servers to start their clearing duties on the sanctuary. This 6 minutes had to elapse before the altar servers leading the procession had reached the priests' sacristy when they bowed to the crucifix at the end of their procession, and before they commenced their duties ferrying sacred items from the sanctuary to the priests' sacristy.

So here was the problem. J claimed that he and R were ferreting around and were 'in the room a couple of minutes maximum before Pell came in'. But on the final version put the jury, they had already spent at least 5 ½ minutes on the convoluted new route getting to the sacristy in the first place. Mind you, it would have taken them longer than that because J said they were poking around various places before they got to the priests' sacristy. You'd wonder what the two boys would have discussed with each other before they started their poking around and as they backtracked the 122 steps from the toilet corridor to the south transept and into the priests' sacristy.

Back in Rome, the change of the procession route was the matter which most concerned Detective Superintendent Sheridan. It was the only matter on which he took over from Detective Sergeant Reed during the interview seeking clarification that indeed the usual practice when the weather was fine was for Pell to process down the centre aisle and then to process externally after having stopped for a considerable period of time greeting parishioners on the cathedral steps at the West Door. Sheridan realised that there were problems with J's account of the internal procession. As it turned out, there were to be even greater problems with an amended account of an external procession that swallowed up all the available time for the offending to have occurred. One can only speculate whether Detective Superintendent Sheridan was thereafter unhesitatingly prepared to run with J's account after these warning lights started flashing.

The final route proposed by J not only swallowed up all the possible time for the sacristan Potter to wait before instructing his minions to commence ferrying items from the sanctuary. It created all sorts of imponderables. How would two 13 year-old boys with no previous planning decide to head off on such a convoluted route? Why wouldn't they have simply continued to the end of the toilet corridor turning left and commencing their ferreting, taking just 22 steps down the corridor which was all so familiar to them, given that they went up and back along that corridor every Sunday as J had told the police during the walk-through in March 2016? What made them think they would not have been sprung upon entering a sacristy which was decidedly off-limits to the choir?

For most if not all of the 6 minutes during which Potter was allowing time for people to say their prayers after mass, J and his companion were not walking directly to the priests' sacristy via the 56 step internal procession, they were on a convoluted outside procession and cutback of 408 steps which would have taken them at least 5 ½ minutes before you factor in the additional couple of minutes for ferreting around, finding the wine and swigging it.

3. Greeting on the Steps

Pell also told the police at the record of interview that his practice was to greet congregants on the steps at the west door after mass. In his record of interview, Pell said, 'I mean let me - let me start to roll out – most things on these or this story is counter factual and with a bit of luck I'll be able to demonstrate point by point. The first thing is that after every mass I would stay out at the front of the cathedral and talk to people.' The prosecution willingly conceded that this protocol might have developed later in Pell's ministry but they questioned whether Pell would have spent very long on the steps after his first two solemn masses as archbishop at 11am on the Sunday. Anyone with experience of these things knows that the new archbishop once he stopped on the steps to greet people would have been besieged by his new parishioners. At his first couple of masses, he would have been more likely to spend more time rather than less greeting those keen to meet their new pastor.

If in any doubt about Pell's style and practice at this time, just consider the two page feature done on Pell in the Melbourne *Age* the month before these critical masses. Karen Kissane ended her 4,000 word article *The Gospel According to George* describing Pell after a funeral mass at Fawkner parish:

> After the service they spill on to the concrete outside and the older Italians line up in front of Pell to pay their respects. They reach for his hand, then bend and kiss his knuckles or his ring in an ancient gesture of homage. Some wipe away tears. Pell is unsurprised and responds to each one with a few words or a blessing. Later, when he tries to pose for a photograph, he is surrounded by a flock of giggling nonnas half his size who want to get in the picture too. They are quite unembarrassed; he is their archbishop, the face of their church, and he belongs to them. This is Catholic faith in the old style, ritualised, tribalised and unquestioning.[98]

Every minute Pell spent on those steps after the 11am mass further blew out of the water the prosecution theory that Pell could have been back in the sacristy within 6 minutes of leaving the sanctuary. Even if he'd proceeded directly from the sanctuary without stopping to greet

---

[98] Karen Kissane, 'The Gospel According to George', *The Age*, Saturday Extra, 30 November 1996

a single parishioner, he would have needed to take 308 steps over a 4 ½ minute period which would have commenced after everyone else had processed before him, including 60 members of the choir and a handful of altar servers. You will appreciate that the person at the rear of a procession of at least 70 people processing in twos arrives at the final destination some time after those at the head of the procession. Neither Pell nor J would have made it to the sacristy within the private prayer time, even if that time ran for 6 minutes rather than 2 minutes at most as Mallinson had testified.

One day when visiting the cathedral taking measurements, I was told by the MC that the archbishop leaves the sacristy at 10.54am precisely, when celebrating the 11am mass. So it usually takes the archbishop and his entourage up to 6 minutes to process at the beginning of mass from the sacristy to the west door of the cathedral. The procession of choristers, servers, concelebrants and archbishop would take the same time to return.

4. Accompanied by MC Portelli

Pell also told the police at the record of interview in Rome that he would have been accompanied at all relevant times by his MC Monsignor Portelli. The prosecution investigated a couple of strategies to separate Pell and Portelli for the critical 6 minutes needed for the offending to occur.

The first strategy took up Portelli's admission that if there was another commitment for the archbishop in the cathedral that afternoon, Portelli might have taken a couple of minutes to reorder the archbishop's speaking notes and liturgical books back at the lectern on the sanctuary. But there were no such scheduled events on these days. It was suggested that the archbishop might have celebrated the evening mass at the cathedral and that might have required Portelli to prepare papers at the lectern. There was no evidence of that. When the archbishop celebrates the main solemn mass in the cathedral on a Sunday he does not return to celebrate the lowkey evening mass. In any event such an absence would account only for a couple of minutes absence.

A second strategy was attempted unsuccessfully at both trials. The prosecution suggested that Portelli might have ducked out for a smoke while being fully vested himself and while the archbishop was still in procession at the end of mass or while the archbishop was on the steps greeting parishioners. Both times, the prosecutor had to retract the suggestion before the jury and apologise. Not only was there no evidence to support the suggestion, the only evidence excluded all possibility of the suggestion. The suggestion was put directly to Portelli by the prosecutor and he denied it. For example at the second trial, the prosecutor asked Portelli:

> You said you were a 20 cigarettes a day man, mass has been for over an hour, you didn't go outside to have a smoke after mass?
>
> ---It would be as appropriate as for instance His Honour walking down William Street dressed as he is smoking a cigarette, which is not done.[99]

When the prosecutor put the suggestion to the jury a second time, this was the indication as to just how difficult it was for the prosecution to find those magical 6 minutes when Pell could be alone together with the two boys in the sacristy.

THE FIFTH CHARGE – the thirteenth stroke of the clock

The main incident alleged in the Pell proceedings gave rise to four charges. I should say a word about the fifth charge which was truly preposterous. It relates to an incident alleged to have occurred two months after the first incident, in the crowded sacristy corridor as the choir and servers were processing together. Like the thirteenth stroke of a clock, J's account of this incident should have alarmed and alerted police, prosecutors and judges that not all was well with J's recollection of events. The allegation was that Pell having presided at a mass

---

[99] *Director of Public Prosecutions v. George Pell,* Transcript of Proceedings, p. 591, 20 November 2018.

celebrated by Fr Brendan Egan had been at the rear of the procession at the end of mass, immediately behind Fr Egan. Pell had split from the procession and gone forward with many people congregated in the corridor, pinning J to the wall and sexually assaulting him. Here is the High Court's description:

The assumption that a group of choristers, including adults, might have been so preoccupied with making their way to the robing room as to fail to notice the extraordinary sight of the Archbishop of Melbourne dressed 'in his full regalia' advancing through the procession and pinning a 13 year old boy to the wall, is a large one. The failure to make any formal report of such an incident, had it occurred, may be another matter.

It is unnecessary to decide whether J's description of the second incident so strains credulity as to necessitate that the jury, who saw and heard him give the evidence, ought to have entertained a reasonable doubt as to its occurrence. The capacity of the evidence to support the verdict on this charge suffers from the same deficiency as the evidence of the assaults involved in the first incident.[100]

If this charge were to be brought, you would think the police would want to lead evidence from Brendan Egan. You would think they would try and track down any others who would have been in the corridor that day. Here is the shocking thing. To this day, the police have never even spoken to Egan. Egan left the priesthood some years ago, but he was in gainful employment with a local council in Melbourne during the course of the legal proceedings and readily contactable. And there is no 'record of anyone undertaking any investigation about J's allegations' in relation to this incident. Here is Richter's cross-examination of Detective Sergeant Reed who was in charge of the 'investigation':[101]

All right. We then go to Sunday 23 February?

---

[100] *Pell* v *The Queen* (2020) 258 CLR 123, 165-6
[101] *Director of Public Prosecutions v. George Pell*, Transcript of Proceedings, p. 1249, 29 November 2018

---Yes.

Which is the only entry, of February, in the Connor diary, that has Archbishop Pell presiding. Right?

---Ah, for February, yes.

Right. Now, if you were investigating that occasion as a possibility?

---yes.

That Archbishop Pell is supposed to pushed Mr J into the wall and grabbed his private parts, and squeezed them hard, you'd want to speak to Father Brendan Egan, wouldn't you?

---Father Egan hasn't been spoken to.

Why?

---Ah, I don't have an answer for that. Because I haven't spoken to him.

You see, because you'd want to know, from Father Egan, whether he went back in procession with Archbishop Pell, who had been presiding. You'd want to know that, wouldn't you?

---Yes, that would be reasonable. Yes.

You'd want to know whether they disrobed together, in the sacristy?

---Yes. That would be reasonable.

Okay. So, no enquiries have been made in relation to February of 1997 at all that relate to this allegation? Of the second episode?

---No. Not in relation to Father Egan they haven't, no.

No?

---No.

But in relation to anything that would provide any evidence about an alleged episode in February of '97?

---No investigations undertaken by me, no. The evidence that has been given is the only material.

Thank you. And when you say "not by me," you were the leader of the team and interposed, contains all the activities of the team - - ?

---No, it doesn't. I didn't say that.

Well, is there any record of anyone undertaking any investigation about J's allegations relating to February 1997?

---No. Not that I'm - not that I can categorically recall now. No.

Well, not that you recall at all?

---Not that I can recall, no.

Right. And if there had been, you'd have known about it?

---Yes, you would.

Yes. Thank you.

In the absence of any evidence from Egan or any person other than J who would have been present in that corridor, Chief Justice Ferguson and President Maxwell, impressed by J's demeanour, accepted that this assault had been proved beyond reasonable doubt. Their Honours wrote:[102]

> Nor do we regard the description of the second incident as being so improbable as to entail a reasonable doubt. ...[A] fleeting physical encounter of the kind described by J can be readily imagined. Jurors would know from common experience that confined spaces facilitate furtive sexual touching, even when others are in the same space. And the act of squeezing the genitals is, itself, unremarkable as a form of sexual assault. On J's account, this was opportunistic offending, just as the first incident had been. On this occasion, however, it was over almost immediately. As he said in evidence-in-chief: 'Just a quick, he squeezed and kept walking. It was something that was a complete and utter whirlwind. It was very quick.'
>
> What does seem improbable to us — referring again to the defence's 'fabrication' hypothesis — is that J would have thought to invent a

---

[102] *George Pell v The Queen* [2019] VSCA 186, ##112-3.

second incident if his true purpose was to advance false allegations against Cardinal Pell. Having to construct and maintain a story of a second and subsequent assault could only have made the undertaking much more difficult and risky for J, markedly increasing the likelihood that the whole story would unravel when tested.

Justice Weinberg in dissent observed:[103]

> Objectively speaking, this was always going to be a problematic case. The complainant's allegations against the applicant were, to one degree or another, implausible. In the case of the second incident, even that is an understatement.

> That is not so by reason of the complainant having alleged that he had been sexually abused, in the past, by a senior Catholic cleric. Sadly, as we have come to appreciate, there is nothing wholly improbable about allegations of that kind being true. It is, rather, by reason of the detailed circumstances that were said to have surrounded those allegations of abuse, circumstances as to time, place and manner.

Lord Atkin once wrote: 'An ounce of intrinsic merit or demerit in the evidence, that is to say the value of the comparison of evidence with known facts, is worth pounds of demeanour'.[104] Having assessed the intrinsic merit of the scant evidence available on the fifth charge, Justice Weinberg and all seven Justices of the High Court had no hesitation in acquitting Pell of this charge. If the DPP were to proceed with this charge, and if the police were to propose this allegation for prosecution, they should at least have ensured that Egan was spoken to, if not called as a witness. It's a farce that the policeman in charge of the investigation had to answer under oath that there was absolutely no 'record of anyone undertaking any investigation about J's allegations relating to February 1997'.

---

[103] *George Pell* v *The Queen* [2019] VSCA 186, ##1054-5.
[104] Lord Atkin in *Société d'avances Commerciales (Société Anomyne Egyptienne)* v *Merchants' Marine Insurance Co. ('The Palitana')* (1924) 20 Lloyds L Rep 140, 152.

CONCLUSION

I've said enough to indicate why no one can seriously question the conclusion of the 7 High Court judges. Let me quote to you again their conclusion:

> 'It remains that the evidence of witnesses, whose honesty was not in question, (i) placed (Pell) on the steps of the Cathedral for at least ten minutes after Mass on 15 and 22 December 1996; (ii) placed him in the company of Portelli when he returned to the priests' sacristy to remove his vestments; and (iii) described continuous traffic into and out of the priests' sacristy for ten to 15 minutes after the altar servers completed their bows to the crucifix.'[105]

Chief Justice Ferguson and Justice Maxwell denied the validity of this conclusion. By way of contrast, here is what Ferguson and Maxwell concluded:[106]

> In our view, taking the evidence as a whole, it was open to the jury to find that the assaults took place in the 5-6 minutes of private prayer time and that this was before the 'hive of activity' described by the other witnesses began. The jury were not bound to have a reasonable doubt.

The High Court rightly concluded that on the overwhelming weight of evidence neither Pell nor the two boys could have been in the sacristy during those 6 minutes. The boys were processing and back-tracking and ferreting; Pell was processing down the main aisle and out on the steps greeting his new parishioners.

Upon the analysis of the High Court and consistent with the painstaking review of the totality of the evidence by the dissenting Justice Weinberg in the Victorian Court of Appeal, there was not the evidence to convict Pell on any of these charges. Since the High Court decision, no one has come up with even a credible theory as to how Pell

---

[105] *Pell* v *The Queen* (2020) 258 CLR 123, 164
[106] *George Pell* v *The Queen* [2019] VSCA 186, #300 [The Victorian Court of Appeal decision has not been reported in the authorised *Victorian Reports*].

and two choir boys could be alone together completely uninterrupted for 6 minutes in the priests' sacristy soon after mass and before choir rehearsals for the Christmas concert. If the police had their doubts about the statements of Pell, Portelli and Potter, on their return from Rome in October 2016 they should have sought out and spoken to any altar servers, money collectors and concelebrants who would have been there, before instituting committal proceedings 18 months later. In the Rome interview, Pell had provided the police with an inconvenient truth: J's account was just not credible. But, undaunted by this inconvenient truth, the police returned to Melbourne and pursued their unsustainable case theory.

None of us knows the identity of the complainant, nor should we. When the High Court acquitted Cardinal Pell of all charges, J issued a statement through his lawyer Vivian Waller saying: 'My journey has been long and I am relieved that it is over. I have my ups and downs. The darkness is never far away. Despite the stress of the legal process and public controversy I have tried hard to keep myself together. I am OK. I hope that everyone who has followed this case is OK.' Earlier, Vivian Waller told Louise Milligan that J has 'experienced depression, loneliness struggle with various issues over time' and that 'the criminal process has been quite stressful for him'.[107] Undoubtedly he has suffered additional trauma through the processes of the law, including the appeals all the way to the High Court. Much of it was avoidable. These processes have also re-traumatised many other people who have experienced institutional child sexual abuse and who have placed hope in our legal system. Their situation would have been assisted if the police in this case had undertaken competent policing.

These failures in due process exposed J to needless and avoidable harm and imposed the grossest injustice on Cardinal Pell. From the moment VicPol laid charges, the reality was that Pell had to prove his innocence to the public. VicPol knew that the mere laying of these charges against Pell would devastate, if not destroy his reputation, in

---

[107] ABC *4 Corners* 'The Conviction of Cardinal Pell', 4 March 1989 available at https://www.abc.net.au/4corners/guilty:-the-conviction-of-cardinal-pell/10869116

the community. In part, VicPol therefore bears the responsibility for the appalling scenes of vitriol and abuse outside the County Court after Pell's conviction became known.

Everything said by the High Court and by Justice Weinberg vindicates the claims made by Pell in his record of interview, particularly his claims about an external procession, his greeting parishioners on the steps, his being accompanied by his MC, and the sacristy being a hive of activity. If only the police had subjected J's recollections and claims to closer scrutiny after learning these recollections of Pell about his usual practice at the cathedral. If only they'd interviewed some of the altar servers. If only they had tracked down and interviewed some of the money collectors and concelebrants. With competent policing, there would have been no need for these trials and appeals.

If only the DPP had insisted that the police provide a brief of evidence capable of countering not only Pell's account, but also the claims made by a string of opportunity witnesses who honestly recalled to the best of their ability what went on at the cathedral during the busiest time of the week. The DPP has a policy that it 'not put forward theories that are not supported by evidence'[108]. By the time the case got to the High Court, the DPP appearing in person did put forward theories not supported by the evidence. Kerri Judd QC asserted wrongly that the altar servers adjourned to the 'worker sacristy' for the critical minutes, and that the private prayer time might have been much more than 6 minutes. There was no evidence for either proposition. She even submitted that the matter should be remitted to the Victorian Court of Appeal because the High Court did not 'have before it the material to enable it to determine whether the verdicts are unreasonable or cannot be supported by the evidence'. In its judgment, the High Court described this submission with one word: 'specious'[109]. The Pell saga reminds us that we should be grateful that we live in a federation with

---

[108] *Policy of the Director of Public Prosecutions for Victoria,* authorised by K Judd QC, 18 January 2021, p. 8, available at https://www.opp.vic.gov.au/getattachment/a26fab55-0c8a-48a9-b4e5-71f3a898e6cb/DPP-Policy.aspx

[109] *Pell* v *The Queen* (2020) 258 CLR 123, 137. Equally 'specious' was the DPP's submission that the matter be 'relisted before this Court so that the whole of the evidence might be placed before it.'

the High Court of Australia overseeing the criminal justice systems of the states and territories. It was specious to suggest that the Pell matter be referred back to the Victorian criminal justice system.

When Cardinal Pell walked free from prison, he said, 'I hold no ill will toward my accuser, I do not want my acquittal to add to the hurt and bitterness so many feel; there is certainly hurt and bitterness enough. The only basis for long term healing is truth and the only basis for justice is truth, because justice means truth for all.' I hope my book and these remarks contribute to justice, truth and healing.

About the Author

Fr Frank Brennan SJ AO is Rector of Newman College at the University of Melbourne. He is a Distinguished Fellow of the PM Glynn Institute at Australian Catholic University and an Adjunct Professor at the Thomas More Law School at ACU. He has been appointed a peritus at the Catholic Church's Fifth Plenary Council of Australia. He is the author of numerous books on human rights having chaired the Australian Government's 2009 National Human Rights Consultation and having been a member of the Australian Government's 2018 Religious Freedom Review. Most recently he has served on the Australian Government's Senior Advisory Group designing a proposed 'Indigenous Voice' for the First Nations Peoples in Australia.

Lightning Source UK Ltd.
Milton Keynes UK
UKHW021451230522
403390UK00007B/1113